Frame It!

EASY FRAMING IDEAS & TECHNIQUES FOR ABSOLUTELY ANYTHING

BY TONIA DAVENPORT

NORTH LIGHT BOOKS
Cincinnati, Ohio
www.artistsnetwork.com

ABOUT THE AUTHOR

Tonia is currently an editor on the craft team at North Light Books. Before becoming an editor, she worked as a professional picture framer for 10 years. Tonia graduated from Western Washington University, where she majored in Visual Communications. For the last several years, she has enjoyed success as a freelance artist, and she has taught workshops on bookbinding and framing. Her artistic endeavors include abstract painting and assemblage, and she enjoys many different crafts including metal crafts, stained glass, papercrafts and fiber arts. Tonia lives in Mason, Ohio, with her husband, Dave, five cats and two dogs.

Frame It! Copyright © 2005 by Tonia Davenport. Manufactured in China. All rights reserved. The patterns and drawings in the book are for the personal use of the reader. By permission of the author and publisher, they may be either hand-traced or photocopied to make single copies, but under no circumstances may they be resold or republished. It is permissible for the purchaser to make the projects contained herein and sell them at fairs, bazaars and craft shows. No other part of this book may be reproduced in any form or by any electronic or mechanical means including information storage and retrieval systems without permission in writing from the publisher, except by a reviewer, who may quote a brief passage in review. Published by North Light Books, an imprint of F+W Publications, Inc., 4700 East Galbraith Road, Cincinnati, Ohio 45236. (800) 289-0963. First edition.

09 08 07 06 05   5 4 3 2 1

Distributed in Canada by Fraser Direct
100 Armstrong Avenue
Georgetown, ON, Canada L7G 5S4
Tel: (905) 877-4411

Distributed in the U.K. and Europe by David & Charles
Brunel House, Newton Abbot, Devon, TQ12 4PU, England
Tel: (+44) 1626 323200, Fax: (+44) 1626 323319
Email: mail@davidandcharles.co.uk

Distributed in Australia by Capricorn Link
P.O. Box 704, S. Windsor, NSW 2756 Australia
Tel: (02) 4577-3555

Library of Congress Cataloging-in-Publication Data
Davenport, Tonia
Frame it : easy framing ideas and techniques for absolutely anything
/ Tonia Davenport.
p. cm.
ISBN 1-58180-688-4 (alk. paper)
1. Picture frames and framing. I. Title.
TT899.2.D38 2005
749'.7--dc22   2005003883

Editor: Christine Doyle
Designer: Marissa Bowers and StanardDesign Partners
Production Coordinator: Robin Richie
Photographer: Christine Polomsky, Tim Grondin and Greg Grosse
Photo Stylist: Jan Nickum

METRIC CONVERSION CHART

To convert	to	multiply by
Inches	Centimeters	2.54
Centimeters	Inches	0.4
Feet	Centimeters	30.5
Centimeters	Feet	0.03
Yards	Meters	0.9
Meters	Yards	1.1
Sq. Inches	Sq. Centimeters	6.45
Sq. Centimeters	Sq. Inches	0.16
Sq. Feet	Sq. Meters	0.09
Sq. Meters	Sq. Feet	10.8
Sq. Yards	Sq. Meters	0.8
Sq. Meters	Sq. Yards	1.2
Pounds	Kilograms	0.45
Kilograms	Pounds	2.2
Ounces	Grams	28.3
Grams	Ounces	0.035

DEDICATION

Mom, I have to dedicate this book to you. You have always made me feel like I was someone special and capable of doing just about anything. Thanks for giving me the confidence I need to succeed. You are at the root of all of my creative inspiration, and my fondest memories involving creativity are the ones of us creating things together.

ACKNOWLEDGMENTS

I could not have done this book without the tremendous support from my editor, Christine Doyle, who continually looks out for my best interest, and from my North Light family in general. Thanks to Tricia Waddell for believing in my ability to do a book, and to all the others who touched the book along the process, including Christine Polomsky, Marissa Bowers, Tim Grondin, Jan Nickum, Cynthia Stanard and Robin Richie.

Thank you also to Lyn Dipasquale from Frame Concepts, Linda McClellan from Nielsen Bainbridge and Brian Buell from Logan Graphic Products, Inc. All of your contributions helped me out considerably.

TABLE OF Contents

Introduction   6

The Frame Package   8

Framing Techniques   13

Traditional Framing Solutions   30

FRAMING SOLUTION NO. 1:

Decorating a Mat Using a Tape Mask   32

FRAMING SOLUTION NO. 2:

Mounting a Textile   36

FRAMING SOLUTION NO. 3:

Reducing the Size of a Premade Frame   42

FRAMING SOLUTION NO. 4:

Cutting a Multi-Opening Mat   46

FRAMING SOLUTION NO. 5:

Creating a Folded-Side Shadow Box   52

FRAMING SOLUTION NO. 6:

Wrapping a Mat with Fabric   58

FRAMING SOLUTION NO. 7:

Cutting Decorative Mat Corners   64

FRAMING SOLUTION NO. 8:

Adapting a Ready-Made Frame
to Be a Shadow Box   68

FRAMING SOLUTION NO. 9:

Using a Fillet as a Frame   74

FRAMING SOLUTION NO. 10:

Mounting Collectibles   78

FRAMING SOLUTION NO. 11:

Creating Depth With Trim Molding   84

Alternative Framing Solutions   88

FRAMING SOLUTION NO.12:

Creating a Glass Pocket with Nails   90

FRAMING SOLUTION NO.13:

Securing an Image to a Board with Acrylic   94

FRAMING SOLUTION NO.14:

Creating a Vinyl Pocket on Fabric   98

FRAMING SOLUTION NO.15:

Using a Clipboard as a Frame   102

FRAMING SOLUTION NO.16:

Creating an Acrylic Box for Dimensional Art   106

FRAMING SOLUTION NO.17:

Mounting a Double-Sided Image   110

FRAMING SOLUTION NO.18:

Creating a Nonmitered Frame   114

FRAMING SOLUTION NO.19:

Using Hardware Pieces to Create a Frame   118

FRAMING SOLUTION NO.20:

Building a Frame Around an Acrylic Box   122

Resources   126
Index   127

Introduction

Some people think of framing as interior decorating. I think of framing as journaling for your walls.

When friends come into my house they see expressions of what I love, places I've been and things I've experienced. You can learn quite a bit about me by looking at my walls. I can count on one hand (or maybe even half a hand) the number of poster prints I've framed for myself. Instead, I've framed a Seattle's Best Coffee bag (and some beans), a brochure from Buca di Beppo, a Polaroid of my first house under construction, snowmen postage stamps, the front page of the *Cincinnati Enquirer* from January 1, 2000, my wedding invitation (and some photos), tickets from a Roaring Camp narrow-gauge railroad trip and so many other miscellaneous things. I can't help myself. I love being reminded daily of the many good times I've had. Even if you're not into saving mementos from events and places like I am, what you consider worthy of having up on your wall speaks of where your passions lie and sometimes even what you dream of (which says something about you, too). Don't ever feel silly about framing something that others might not consider as having monetary value. If it means something to you, makes you remember a happy experience or just makes you smile, it's worth framing.

The neat thing about framing is that you can participate in the process at any level you feel comfortable. Most people assume you have two choices when it comes to getting something framed: one, you can take your artwork into the local frame gallery and have a professional complete the project in its entirety; or two, you can order all of your own materials and then cut, join and fit everything yourself. But there are far more options than just those two. You could cut your own mat, but have a frame shop complete the frame and fit it for you. You could have a professional cut your mat, but cut and join your own frame. You could order a frame from a gallery, already cut to size, and then join it yourself. You could buy a ready-made frame that suits your artwork, and then either have a professional cut a mat for you to fit in the frame, or cut your own . . . you get the idea.

This book is all about showing you those different options. At the same time, together we can explore creative techniques for framing that you may never have even seen before, let alone considered you could do yourself. You may get inspired to frame a favorite toy from childhood, the collection of wine corks you have in the kitchen drawer, or your grandmother's high school diploma that your mother has been keeping in an envelope up in her closet.

Are the wheels turning yet? One word of warning: Framing can be highly addictive. Ready?

WHAT IS A FRAMING SOLUTION?

In this book, framing solutions are presented to you in the form of twenty unique projects. Each project is an example of how to solve a typical framing concern. Do you want to mount a dimensional object? Cut a mat with multiple openings? Figure out how to avoid using a frame altogther? These concerns and more that relate to both the aesthetic and structural components of a framing project are shown. But these ideas are just a glimpse of what you can achieve with framing. Combine, substitute and adapt any of these solutions to come up with a plan that works for you and your own specific item.

The Frame Package

The frame package refers to the sum of everything that goes into or is attached to the outside of the frame itself. This includes the glazing (glass), mat board or spacer, artwork, backing, dust cover and hanging hardware. Traditionally, the package works to seal and protect the artwork, while the frame provides an attractive housing for everything.

Following are examples and descriptions of what you should consider when choosing materials for your framing package.

MAT BOARD

The purpose of a window mat, cut from mat board, is twofold. First, it provides protection by acting as a barrier between the artwork and the glass. Its second purpose is to add aesthetic value. A border around your artwork creates a nice spot for your eye to rest between the artwork and the frame. Sometimes things that aren't matted can appear a little crowded in the frame.

Following are the basic types of mat board available. There is a dizzying amount of choice when you add up all of the varieties and the colors available within each variety. Mat board comes in several different plies, or thicknesses. The most common are 4-ply, which is about $1/16$" (2mm) thick and 8-ply, which comes out to about $1/8$" (3mm).

White Core

The core material for this type of 4-ply mat is bleached a bright white. Because the product is typically cotton, rather than paper, you never have to worry about the bevel (the exposed cut edge) turning brown or yellow. The crisp white will last forever. The colored paper mounted on the top of these mats comes in hundreds of colors.

Black Core

The core material in these boards is black, while the paper mounted on top of them comes in a wide variety of colors. The result is a white or colored mat with a black bevel. Black-core mats are now available in acid-free versions. I like to use these mats on artwork that contains text or fine black linework, to really pull out the detail.

Museum Board or Rag Board

Acid-free and lignin-free, rag mat board is a cotton product that is far superior to the paper mats of the past. This type of matting is the same color all the way through. The biggest selection of these mats is in the neutral tones, but more and more colors are becoming available all the time. I like using museum boards in a soft color when I don't want to see a bright-white bevel. This type of mat can't be beat for its archival properties, particularly the Artcare boards from Bainbridge, whose mats not only won't harm your artwork, but will actively protect your artwork by neutralizing other acids present in the frame and the art itself. Some boards have been given an extra smooth surface, like the Artcare Vellums, making them the best option for adding French lines or other decorative elements.

TERM TO KNOW:
Artwork

In this book (as well as in the framing industry in general), you will find the term artwork used to refer to anything that you are planning to put in a frame. This term applies whether it is fine art or a collection of bottle caps.

8-Ply

This ultra-thick mat is the equivalent of two 4-ply mats mounted together. The result is an extra-wide bevel. These mats are most often museum boards (a solid color throughout) but there are some solid colors with white bevels and whites with a black bevel available as well.

Fabric

This is a mat that has had fabric mounted on the top, and offers a way to have a fabric mat without hand-wrapping one. Leather, silk and suede mats are available as well as many styles of linen. These mats are typically no more difficult to cut than a standard white-core mat.

Metallic

Another version of the white-core (and sometimes black-core) mat is a metal-lic mat. Available in numerous finishes, textures and colors, I think these mats work best as a reveal (middle or bottom mat) rather than as a top mat.

Textured/Patterned

Some textures are merely printed on the top layer of the paper, while some mats are actually embossed. Everything from spatter to leaves to stripes is available in this category.

TERM TO KNOW: *Reveal*

When you have more than one window mat on a piece of artwork, the amount that you see of the mat (or mats) stacked below the top mat is referred to as the reveal. The most common amounts to show are $\frac{1}{8}$" (3mm), $\frac{3}{16}$" (5mm) and $\frac{1}{4}$" (6mm), but any amount is possible.

BACKING

Whatever it is you are framing, you are going to need some sort of backing behind the artwork to hold it into the frame. The amount of space left over after glass, matting and artwork often dictates which backing to use.

Regular Foam Board

Most commonly available in $\frac{1}{8}$" (3mm) and $\frac{3}{16}$" (5mm) thicknesses, this board is the best choice for spray mounting, or as a less-expensive alternative to acid-free foam board.

Acid-Free Foam Board

Available in the same thicknesses as regular foam board, this version contains no harmful elements.

Adhesive-Backed Mounting Board

This board is available in both regular and acid-free varieties and several thicknesses. It has adhesive on one side with a peel-off backing and is a nice, clean way to mount something flat without the use of a spray.

4-Ply Mat Board

The same mat board described earlier can also serve as a backing if you're running low on frame space.

From left to right: black core, chenille fabric, striped patterned, suede fabric, white core, and embossed textured mat boards.

TAPES, CORNERS AND ADHESIVES

There are several types of tape and other adhesives that are good to have on hand before beginning any framing project. Consider not only archival properties in your adhesives, but also holding power.

Adhesive Transfer Tape

This product can be applied either with or without a tape gun and is primarily used to adhere layers of mat board together. Think of it as a thin layer of rubber cement that has dried to the tacky stage. It is available in regular and acid-free versions, as well as several widths. It is applied by pressing the tape against the surface and pulling off the brown paper backing. While similar to double-sided tape, adhesive transfer tape is much less expensive. Look for it at art supply and framing stores.

Framer's and Artist's Tape

Almost all of these tapes are pH-neutral or acid-free and are used to mount artwork to a backing, as well as to hinge a mat to the backing. I think these tapes are the easiest to work with for mounting purposes, if you're not concerned by placing tape on the artwork.

Gummed Linen Tape

Activated with water, like a mailing envelope, this type of tape is archival and easily reversible with more moisture. One con to this tape, however: it tends to dry out more easily over time than framer's or artist's tape and lose its adhesive hold.

Acid-Free Photo Corners

These clear, soft plastic corners are ideal for the times when you don't want any adhesive touching your artwork and when your art will be protected by a window mat. Photo corners are also the best choice if you know you will remove your artwork from the backing at some point. While there are several sizes available, including 3" (8cm) ones for mounting large limited edition prints, I prefer using photo corners only on pieces of art 11" x 14" (28cm x 36cm) or smaller and a 1¼" (3cm) size works well for most applications.

Archival Glue

Similar to white craft glue, archival glue is nice to have on hand for attaching small embellishments or to use when floating (see page 13) a large, heavy piece of watercolor paper.

Spray Adhesive

This is fine for mounting anything that you are not overly concerned about protecting for long periods. It is not archival and can be a bit messy, but it can't be beat for a quick fix. It nicely keeps a poster flat and wave-free, and it's also ideal for mounting fabric or decorative paper to a mat board.

Silicone

Silicone is the type of adhesive to use when mounting heavier items in a shadow box project. It's especially suited for nonporous items like a plate or a golf ball. Silicone comes in many different forms and brands, and generally is not exactly acid-free. It will peel off many surfaces if future removal is desired.

GLAZING

The word *glazing* refers to the glass or acrylic piece that you choose to include in your framing package. Single-strength picture framing glass is typically 2.5mm thick and can be purchased from a frame shop cut to order, or you can buy a sheet (known as a *lite* in the industry, if you'd like to impress your local supplier) from a glass company or some hardware stores and cut it yourself. Below is a description of some types of glazing as well as some things to consider before choosing a piece for your framing project.

Regular Glass

This is the most general purpose and cost-effective glazing solution. Regular glass will block 43–47 percent of harmful UV rays from reaching your artwork.

Reflection-Control Glass

Etched on one side, this glass has a satin finish and cuts down significantly on glare. However it also cuts just a bit of clarity. I don't recommend using this glass in any instance where the artwork is set back, away from the glass, like with a triple mat or in a shadow box. This type of glass will keep just over 50 percent of harmful UV rays from the artwork.

Conservation Glass

Available in both clear (which looks like regular glass) and reflection-control, this glass has a coating on one side that blocks 97percent of harmful UV rays from reaching your artwork. I use this type of glass more than any other because what I'm framing is usually

sentimental and I care about preserving it. This type of glass is meant to be cut on the side without the coating. The coated side will scratch if care is not taken, but the coated side also is the one that faces the artwork, so cleaning this type of glass is worry-free.

Anti-Reflective Glass

Although it is a bit pricey and difficult to clean, this glass is almost magical. Tru Vue makes this glass and when viewed straight on, a clean piece appears almost invisible. This is a great glass to use on shadow-box pieces when the elimination of glare is desired. It's especially nice on black pieces, too. Tru Vue claims this glass blocks 78 percent of harmful UV rays from reaching the artwork.

Acrylic

Picture-frame-quality acrylic looks identical to regular glass in almost any frame. It is about half the weight of glass, and I especially like it for creative endeavors because it can be scratched up or drilled into. Look for it in many of the projects in the Alternative Framing Solutions section of this book. Sheets of various sizes can be purchased at the hardware store, and it is very easy to cut down yourself. It is available from frame shops in regular and conservation varieties as well.

From left to right: spray adhesive, photo corners, adhesive transfer tape, artist's tape.

FINISHING HARDWARE

Hardware is the silent partner in holding your framing project together. While not as glamorous as mat board or glass, having the correct hardware available is just as important as any aesthetic element and will save you from searching the medicine cabinet for headache relief.

Finishing Nails

These nails come with very small heads so that you can countersink (hammer in far enough so that the head is below the surface) them easily with a nail set. The 1" and 1½" (3cm and 4cm) sizes should cover all of your general needs. Nail filler or framer's putty can be used to fill the holes made by these nails, if desired.

Framer's Points

These are the specialty brads that go in a point driver. If you don't enjoy hammering traditional nails in the rabbet of a frame (which can sometimes be awkward), a point driver such as the Fletcher Framemaster might be worth considering.

Offset Clips

When the frame package extends outside the back of the frame, offset clips allow you to secure the package to the frame using a stair-step design with a hole in one end to screw into the back of the frame. These clips are available in ⅛", ¼", ⅜" and ½" (3mm, 6mm, 10mm and 13mm) sizes.

Strap Hangers

These pieces have a triangular or D-shaped ring on one end and a flat piece with a hole in it for a screw on the other end. They are screwed into the back of the frame to tie hanging wire onto. There are several sizes and strengths available, depending on the width of your frame and the weight of the finished project.

Wood Screws

A good, all-round size is ⅜" (10mm) x 6 (the six identifies the length of the screw but does not refer to a measurement in inches). These are handy for securing offset clips and strap hangers.

Screw Eyes

If you can't locate strap hangers, or your frame is too narrow to accomodate them, screw eyes will do the trick. It's a good idea to predrill before using larger screw eyes to avoid splitting the wood. Start turning the eye with your fingers, then use a scratch awl or a nail set inserted through the eye to complete the turning. Choose a screw length that can be screwed in deep enough so that the eye is just starting to push into the frame.

Picture Wire

Picture wire comes in several weights and is either coated or uncoated. While the coated version costs a bit more, I think it's worth it because it doesn't draw blood from your fingers nor will it turn them black. Look on the package for correct weight maximums.

Sawtooth Hangers

If your picture isn't too heavy or too large, sawtooth hangers can substitute for hangers and wire. For pictures that are especially long and horizontal, two sawtooth hangers, one on either end, are better than one central hanger. Look for the type that you can hammer in directly, instead of securing with tiny nails. They are much easier to use.

From left to right: sawtooth hangers, offset clips and finishing nails, point driver, picture hanging wire, framer's points and screw eyes. Upper left: strap hangers.

Framing Techniques

The wheels are turning, I can hear them. You've probably got a list of things you'd like to frame, but you're wondering about the know-how required to complete a framing project yourself. Don't worry! Let's take a moment to go over some basic information. I'll walk you through the basic framing process and when we're done, you'll be rushing out the door to gather your materials.

MEASURE TWICE, CUT ONCE

This age-old cliché may sound a bit nagging, but it came into existence for a reason. The reason is that it's a real bummer replacing materials because you cut something too big or too small and you can't make creative adjustments in some instances. Measuring really is quite rudimentary and only takes a small amount of math (oh no!) and a bit of planning.

Adding fractions on a calculator is easy. If you haven't done too much of this in the past and you don't have the conversions memorized, here is a quick reference chart for you to use.

Fractions to Decimals

1/16	.0625	3/8	.375	11/16	.6875
1/8	.125	7/16	.4375	3/4	.75
3/16	.1875	1/2	.5	13/16	.8125
1/4	.25	9/16	.5625	7/8	.875
5/16	.3125	5/8	.625	15/16	.9375

TERM TO KNOW: *Float Mount*

When artwork is set on top of a mat, rather than attached behind a window in a mat, it is said to be floating on the mat. A float mount can be done many different ways. The artwork can be glued down to the mat, sewn onto the mat or taped to the mat.

DETERMINING MAT COLOR

Just about any artwork that you wish to frame is shown off to its best when the eye has a place to rest between the artwork and the frame itself. This is most easily accomplished with the addition of a window mat, but it can also be done by "floating" the artwork on top of a piece of matboard, and leaving an ample amount of space around it (see page 74). Sometimes it is best to combine these two methods (see page 64). Whichever route you choose to take, the first step in framing your piece is to decide the amount of border that will surround your artwork. A factor to consider when planning this amount is color.

Typically, white or light colors work best for larger borders. With dark or more intense colors, a little may go a long way, and a smaller border is often appropriate. A common way to choose colors for your matting is to look at your artwork as a whole. Squint a little if it helps, and see what color is the overall dominant color. This color will usually work best for your main or top mat. If there is another color that you like and it appears more as an accent, or in a smaller amount, try using that color as a reveal or bottom mat.

If you are still undecided, ask a friend to come along for a second opinion and, of course, there is the most obvious solution—ask the person behind the counter for assistance. Framers get to see many different types of artwork, so chances are good that they have seen something quite similar to your piece before and can offer quick help.

As you can see from the four images below, the color of the mat that surrounds your artwork has a significant impact on the overall look of the piece. While none of the options is right or wrong, each does gives the piece a different feel. Each color not only delivers a different mood, but draws attention to different aspects of the artwork.

SIZING THE MAT

Once you've determined your mat color, the next step is to decide on the width of the mat that will best suit the piece. This decision is made easier if you plan to use an appropriately-sized ready-made frame.

TERM TO KNOW:
Weighted Bottom

This term refers to a bottom mat width that is taller or larger than the top and side widths. Sometimes it is desirable to have a dramatic difference in the size of the bottom width compared to the other three sides, but typically only ¼" (6mm) to 1" (3cm) is added. This small difference is usually not detected. The human eye prefers the artwork to be "sitting" on a substantial base (the bottom mat width) and if the bottom width matches the sides, the eye is fooled into seeing the bottom as unsubstantial.

DETERMINING THE MAT WIDTH

When you've decided on a color you like, lay a large piece of it on your worktable and set your artwork on top of it. Use scrap pieces of mat board to figure out how much mat to show around the artwork. Move the loose pieces of mat board until you're satisfied with the size of the mat border.

USING READY-MADE FRAMES TO DETERMINE MAT SIZE

When you know you want to use a standard-size frame, consider these two samples. The skinny mat and smaller frame size on the left would work, but if I increase the mat width and step up to the next standard size (as shown on the right), my images appear much less crowded and the result is far more professional looking.

CHOOSING AND SIZING A FRAME

The actual frame for your artwork is the finishing touch that will create a unified frame package. Following are some tips for choosing a frame style and how to determine the final frame size if you'll be making one yourself.

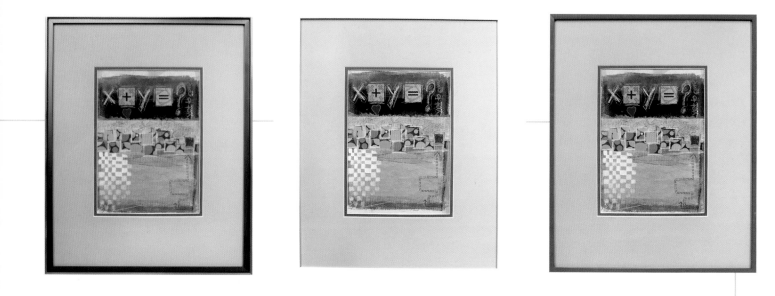

DECIDING ON A FRAME STYLE

The number of frame choices available in either ready-made or custom molding length means that there's a perfect frame for just about any framing project. Here are three frames that all work equally well for this piece of artwork. As with the mats, you can see that the choice of both weight (narrow verses wide) and style (classic verses contemporary) gives a particular feel to the overall piece. There are several things to consider when selecting a frame. Will the artwork be displayed near other framed pieces you already have? Is there a dominant texture in the artwork that could be repeated in the molding? Does the artwork reflect a modern style, or is it more traditional? Can the look of the artwork support a dramatic, wide frame or should the frame line be minimal and simple? One small rule of thumb to keep in mind: the frame width should be approximately one third (at the minimum) larger or smaller than the width of the mat. That is, the two should not be equal.

DETERMINING THE FRAME SIZE

Once you know the border width for each side of your mat, you'll need to determine the width of the entire piece. To do that, double the width of one side of the mat. If applicable, decide on the amount of border you'd like showing around the outside of the artwork, double that and add it to the mat width total. Here, I wanted a mat width on the sides of $3\frac{3}{4}$" (9.5cm), and $\frac{1}{4}$" (6mm) of the white paper to show around the artwork: $3\frac{3}{4} + 3\frac{3}{4} + \frac{1}{4} + \frac{1}{4} = 8$. I set the 8" (20cm) mark at the left side of the artwork, and the measurement at the right side edge is my total frame width size. Repeat for the length (height) of the mat.

CUTTING THE MAT

Once you've determined the mat color and size, the next thing to do is to cut it. Using a contrasting pencil, draw cutting lines on the back of the mat, using the desired mat width measurements. Then use one of the two cutters below to make the cuts.

Handheld Cutter

The use of a handheld cutter is the most economical way to cut your own mat. If you think you may cut up to six mats or so a year, it may be the best choice for you. It takes a bit more practice than using a bench cutter, but typically by the third or fourth mat, a true beginner can be up to speed.

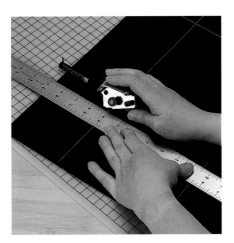

USING A HANDHELD CUTTER AND A STRAIGHTEDGE
Place a cork-backed ruler (the sturdier, the better) to the left side of the first cutting line. Position the cutter ³/₁₆" (5mm) above the horizontal line (or use the guide on your mat cutter). Holding the ruler firmly, push the blade down into the mat and pull the cutter down to the bottom horizontal line, keeping the cutter pushed against the ruler. Repeat on the side parallel to the side you cut, and then on the other two sides using the same method. To make sure your ruler stays firmly in place, you may want to clamp it to your table before cutting.

Bench Cutter

A bench cutter or board-mounted cutter is a bit more of an investment, but it makes the process of cutting a mat almost effortless. There are several levels of quality available, but the results from these cutters are almost perfect every time.

1 SET THE BAR TO THE CORRECT MEASUREMENT
Set the slide bar to the desired mat width. Use a contrasting pencil to mark the cutting lines on all four sides.

2 SLIDE THE HEAD ALONG THE BAR TO CUT
Insert the mat so it's flush against the bar, hold the bar down and make the cut, starting and stopping with the horizontal pencil lines at the guides. (If your cutter doesn't have guides, start and stop the cuts ³/₁₆" (5mm) above and below the horizontal lines.)

CUTTING A DOUBLE MAT

A double mat really sets off a piece of art nicely and tends to make everything look just a bit more "finished." The amount of the bottom mat that shows is referred to as the reveal. The amount of the reveal can be as small as ¹⁄₈" (3mm) for a fine line, or as large as you like, but ³⁄₁₆", ¹⁄₄" and ³⁄₈"(5mm, 6mm and 10mm) are the amounts I prefer and use most often.

DON'T FORGET YOUR SLIP

For a nice clean cut on the bench cutter, place a slip sheet of mat board underneath the mat you're cutting. Each time you make a cut, move the sheet so that you're cutting in a clean part of the slip sheet.

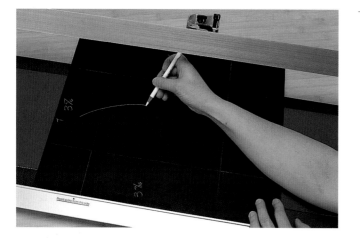

1 | MARK AND CUT THE TOP MAT

Measure and cut your top mat first. When determining the width of the top mat, be sure to factor in the amount of "reveal" you want showing on the second (bottom) mat. For example, if you want your total mat width to be 3" (8cm) and you want to see ¹⁄₄" (6mm) of the bottom mat, cut the top mat at 2³⁄₄" (7cm). Before you remove the top mat from the cutter, draw a line that crosses one of the cuts. This line will serve as a registration mark for the next step.

2 | ADHERE THE MATS TOGETHER

Place adhesive transfer tape along the cut edge of the back of the top mat, making sure not to place the tape over the cut line. Also place tape on the fallout (the piece from the center of the mat). Be sure the fallout is positioned inside of the window the same way it was cut. Use the mark you made in step one for reference. Trim the piece you're going to use as the second (bottom) mat to be about ¹⁄₂" (13m) smaller in each direction than the top mat and center it facedown over the taped top mat. Press down to adhere the two together.

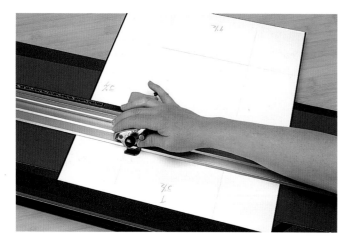

3 | CUT THE BOTTOM MAT

Cut the opening for the second mat using the desired total mat-width measurements. Because the second mat is centered on, and smaller than, the top mat, you'll line the edge of the top mat against the slide bar. After the opening for the second mat is cut, remove the fallout for both mats.

POSITIONING THE ARTWORK

When the placement of your artwork through the window of the mat is critical,
follow these three easy steps to line things up just right.

1 | HINGE THE MAT
Place artist's tape along the top edge of
the backing first. Butt the backing up to
the mat. If the mat is shallower than the
backing, lift the mat up to the tape and
press to adhere.

2 | WEIGHT THE ARTWORK IN PLACE
Fold the mat over, making sure the sides
align. Position the image under the mat
and weight the image with a bag of sand
or rice.

3 | MARK THE CORNERS
Lift the mat up and mark the corners of
where the image will be placed. To make
sure the image doesn't shift as you're
making the marks, hold the image with
your hand.

SECURING THE ARTWORK

Once your artwork is in the correct spot on the backing, you will need to somehow
secure or mount it, to keep it in place. Following are three options for this task:
using a T-hinge, using photo corners and using spray mount.

T-Hinge

Use this quick type of semipermanent mounting for small photos, prints or original
artwork that you don't wish to spray mount. Ideally, an acid-free tape and mounting board should be used. With this option, tape is secured to the back of the artwork, but not to the front.

APPLY TAPE TO THE TOP OF THE ARTWORK
Hinge the mat and mark the corners as shown in steps 1–3
above. Using artist's tape or linen tape, place a piece of tape
under each of the top two corners of the artwork, sticky side up.
Place a second piece of tape perpendicular to each first piece,
lining up the edges with the top edge of the artwork, sticky side
down, securing the first pieces to the mounting board. Burnish
the tape well and close the mat.

Photo Corners

This is the safest way to mount your artwork if it is two-dimensional and not too heavy. Photo corners come in several sizes, and most are acid-free.

THAT HITS THE SPOT

When spray mounting artwork that will have a mat, follow steps 1–3 on page 19 to hinge the mat and mark the corners of the artwork. Use these lines to set your artwork in place after you have sprayed it.

SLIP ON PHOTO CORNERS
Following steps 1–3 on page 19, place the artwork on the backing. Lift up one corner of the artwork, and slip a photo corner over the image. Repeat on all four corners of the image, burnishing the corners as you go. Don't push the corners on too tightly; the artwork needs room to expand and contract with changes in temperature and humidity, or else it will become warped.

Spray Mount

I recommend using spray adhesive only for smaller projects and those you are not sentimental about because this is not an archival means of mounting. Always use in a well-ventilated area that is free of excessive dust.

1 | SPRAY THE BACK OF THE ARTWORK
Place the image facedown on a scrap sheet of paper. Spray adhesive on the back of the image, spraying both horizontally and vertically.

2 | SET THE PIECE IN PLACE
While the spray is still wet, set the artwork carefully down on the backing.

3 | SMOOTH THE ARTWORK DOWN
Place a piece of scrap paper over the image to protect it, then use a brayer to secure the image in place.

CUTTING GLASS

Cutting glass is really not as scary as it sounds. It's a good idea to wear safety glasses when cutting glass to avoid the occasional flying shard. Glass cutters utilize a small wheel that scores the glass so that you can break it. There are several grades of cutters, including those that are disposable, those that accept replaceable wheels and those that house lubricating oil. The amount of glass you're going to be cutting will dictate the type you should own. It is difficult to cut off less than 1" (3cm) of glass, so if you can, start with a piece that is at least a couple of inches bigger in each direction than you need.

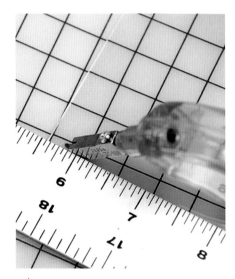

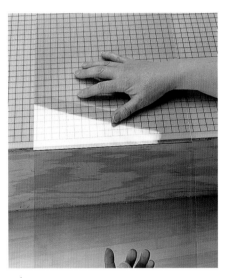

WHAT'S THE SCORE

Score glass on the marked line only once. Trying to rescore on the same line will result in excessive shards and possible chipping, and it will quickly dull the wheel on the cutter.

1 | ALIGN THE CUTTER ON THE MARK
Mark the cuts on the glass with a permanent marker. Align your cutter and cork-backed ruler so that the wheel of the cutter is centered on your cutting mark.

2 | SCORE AND SNAP THE GLASS
Score the glass using the glass cutter (avoid pressing too hard), staying about ⅛" (3mm) away from the top and bottom edges of the glass (to avoid chipping the edge). Place the scored line and excess glass about ⅛" (3mm) off the edge of the table. Hold the glass firmly on the table, then snap the glass down with your other hand to break it on the score line.

GETTING A GRIP

When cutting either glass or acrylic (see page 22), sometimes there is not enough excess to snap using the above method. To snap off a smaller piece, it is necessary to use glass pliers. Hold the main portion of the glazing firmly, and with the pliers gripping the portion that needs to come off, just below the score line, snap the piece off quickly. If only a portion of the excess side breaks off, continue snapping off the remainder of the piece in small bites. The edge may not look pretty, but you should still be able to fit the piece into your frame.

CUTTING MAT CONSERVATION

Dedicate one cutting mat to use for cutting glass or acrylic. The mat will get nicked with the blade of the acrylic cutter and by shards of glass. These nicks can interfere with making smooth cuts on paper, but they won't interfere with scoring glass or acrylic.

CUTTING ACRYLIC

The method to score and cut acrylic is very similar to glass, and in some ways, I think, is easier. One big difference? Glass is scored only once, but when cutting acrylic, the more times you score it, the easier breaking it will be. Use a special plastic cutter, which is sold wherever the acrylic is found. I recommend the cutter by Fletcher, which can be ordered from a frame shop if you can't locate one in the hardware store. If you thought scoring the glass made a chilling sound, wait until you hear the squeal of the plastic cutter!

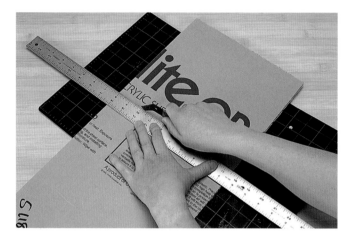

1 | SCORE A LINE
With the protective paper still on the acrylic, measure the width. Use the acrylic scoring tool to score a line in the acrylic. Go over the line 3–4 times, holding the ruler securely in place. It's okay to use firm pressure here.

2 | SNAP THE PIECE APART
Again place the score line and excess acrylic just off the edge of the table and break the acrylic on the score line. This requires a bit more moxie than snapping glass, but if you've scored it enough, it will break away easily.

3 | BREAK THE PAPER IN THE BACK
To break the paper on the back side of the break, bend the pieces the other way, then pull them apart.

CUTTING MOLDING

Picture frame molding can be purchased in length (long strips) from your local frame shop. Most shops will give you a discount for not having to cut the molding themselves, so don't be intimidated to enter a shop with the intention of only ordering a length of molding instead of a full-fledged custom frame job. It is a quick buck for them, and it's a lot cheaper for you. One word of caution: This method of obtaining your molding works best when you need at least 5' (2m). Because the total-length size is determined by the manufacturer, you will be paying for the entire length whether you need it all or not. The frame shop can rarely order less than a full length and will most likely pass the full cost on to you.

Framer's Miter Saw

This Pro Saw, from Logan Graphics, is designed especially for picture frame molding, and cuts very accurately. Similar saws from other manufacturers are available. This is a nice way to go if you want to cut your own frames, you plan on cutting a lot of them, and you don't want to use a power saw.

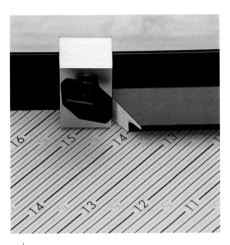

TERM TO KNOW:
Allowance

The frame should always be between $^1/_{16}$" and $^1/_8$" (2mm and 3mm) larger than the frame package (glass, artwork, mat and backing). This is known as an allowance and can be accomplished by either cutting the frame larger than the package, or cutting the package smaller than the frame. Either way, you don't want things too tight.

1 | MAKE THE FIRST CUT
Remeasure the glass to make sure you cut the molding to be $^1/_{16}$" (2mm) larger than the glass (see *Term to Know* at right). To miter the corners, set the saw at 45 degrees and place the first end of the molding about $^1/_4$" (6mm) past the blade. Then use the saw to cut the molding.

2 | TRIM THE FIRST RAIL TO SIZE
Swivel the saw to the other 45 degree side and set the inside of the rail at the desired measurement on the gate. Secure the stop and cut the other end of the rail. Here I am cutting this leg at 14"(36cm).

Miter Box

This is the economy version for the hand-mitered method. This type of saw usually does not come with a gate, so you will need to measure and mark directly on the frame where you need your cuts.

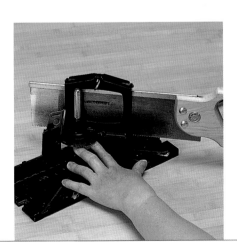

| SECURE THE MOLDING AND CUT
Make the first 45 degree cut and then measure and mark the frame to cut the other end of the rail.

JOINING A FRAME

After all four rails of your frame have been cut, you are ready to glue and nail the pieces together. Any wood glue will serve the purpose, but I prefer a glue that is made especially for picture frames because it will remain slightly flexible when dry. Following are two methods used to secure the pieces of the frame while the glue dries. Experiment to see which method works best for you.

Strap Clamp

Fans of instant gratification will love this system for joining frames. All four corners are glued at once, saving a lot of time.

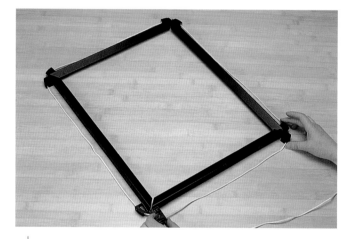

1 | PLACE CORD AND CORNERS AROUND THE FRAME
Loosely assemble the frame on your work surface. Place the four corners of the strap clamp around the corners of the frame.

2 | APPLY GLUE TO THE CORNERS
Remove one short side and place glue on each end. Replace the side and repeat with the other short side.

3 | PULL THE CORD TIGHTLY
Pull the cord tightly to cinch the corners of the frame together. Secure the cord in the wedge of the master corner piece.

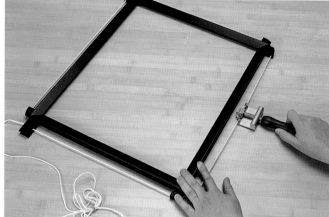

4 | TIGHTEN FURTHER
Make sure each corner is aligned the way you would like, then use the tightening tool to tighten the cord on the side opposite the master corner. Let the frame set until the glue is dry.

Corner Vise

A corner vise set can easily be found at any hardware store. This system works well when the miters on your rails are not perfectly accurate, and joining the pieces may require a little more finagling.

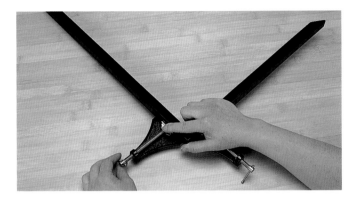

1 SECURE THE FIRST CORNER
Place glue on one end of the short molding. Place the glued end and one long length of cut molding in the clamp. Tighten the vise on each side.

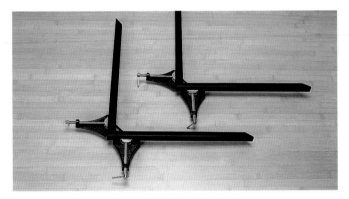

2 SECURE THE OPPOSITE CORNER
Repeat for the other two pieces of molding, making sure you have the long rail and the short rail on the same sides of the vise as the first secured corner.

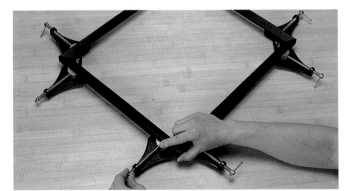

3 COMPLETE THE OTHER TWO CORNERS
Repeat the process to attach to the two halves of the frame together. Set aside for the glue to cure.

MARKER MAGIC

If you have a dark-colored frame, use a marker to color the cut edges of the molding. It will hide minor flaws in the joined corner and will prevent a light-colored wood line.

NAILING THE FRAME

Once the glue in your corners is dry, you are ready to begin nailing the frame. When nailing a corner, be sure the rest of the frame is supported. The number of nails you will need will depend on the frame size and the width and height of the molding. Generally, anything 8" x 10" (20cm x 25cm) or smaller will require just two nails per corner.

1 | CREATE A STARTER HOLE
Clamp the vise to the work table. Place one corner of the frame in the vise, using scrap pieces of mat board to protect the frame from the vise. Make a mark for the nail using the scratch awl.

2 | PREDRILL FOR A NAIL
Use a $^5/_{64}$" (2mm) drill bit to drill a hole at the spot you marked with the awl. Try not to drill in further than two-thirds the length of the nail.

3 | COUNTERSINK THE NAIL
Place a finishing nail in the hole, and pound it all the way in with a hammer. Use the nail set to countersink the nail head into the frame.

4 | FILL HOLES WITH NAIL FILLER
Repeat the process on the other side of the same corner, drilling the hole slightly below or above the hole you just made. Repeat on the three remaining corners. Use wood filler to cover the nail, spreading the filler on with your finger. When the filler is dry, use a marker or paint to cover the wood filler.

PUTTING IT ALL TOGETHER

Now that you have everything cut, taped, glued and nailed, you can begin what's called the *fit*. Fitting is cleaning the glass, putting it with the artwork, securing everything into the frame, sealing the back with a dust cover, and attaching a hanging system.

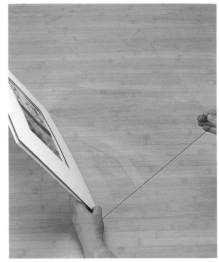

1 | CLEAN THE GLASS
Clean the class with ammonia-free glass cleaner and a terrycloth towel. These towels have less lint than paper towels and you can reuse them. If you are using a lite of acrylic, peel off the first side of the protective backing, but don't remove the other side yet.

2 | CHECK FOR DUST AND LINT
Place the artwork next to the cleaned glass. Use a dusting brush to brush dust from the artwork and the glass. If using acrylic, don't brush the glass, just the artwork. (Acrylic is charged with static and it may actually "suck" dust off of the brush.)

3 | SANDWICH THE ARTWORK AND GLASS
Bring the glass and the artwork together. If you can actually close them together, like you were quickly closing a book, you can blow out even more potential dust.

4 | NAIL IN THE ARTWORK
Make sure there's nothing trapped under the glass. Place the frame on top of the glass and flip the piece over to the back. If you are using a frame that scratches easily, set the inverted frame on a bath towel. Shoot framing points into the frame with the point driver, keeping the driver as level as possible. Apply pressure to the outside of the frame with your other hand to make sure the point driver doesn't force the frame apart.

A GOOD POINT

If you're using a staple gun instead of a point driver, don't place the staple gun right up against the frame. The staple will go all of the way into the wood and will not protrude enough to hold in your frame package. Another economical option for securing artwork is to buy glazier's push points. Use an inserting tool and push the points in by hand.

QUICK SAND

If you're nervous about using a razor blade to trim off the kraft paper, try using a sanding block to sand the paper away from the edge of the frame.

5 | APPLY TAPE TO THE FRAME
Place adhesive transfer tape on the back of the frame, about $\frac{1}{16}$" (2mm) from the outside edge. (You could also use a water-soluble craft or wood glue and smear it on with your finger.)

6 | ADHERE THE DUST COVER
Place a piece of kraft paper or acid-free paper over the tape. Smooth the paper and burnish it onto the tape. Use a razor blade to cut away the excess paper, cutting in about $\frac{1}{16}$" (2mm) from the edge.

7 | MARK HOLES FOR HANGING HARDWARE
From the top of the frame, measure down about one-third of the way, and in the thickest part of the width of the frame, make a mark with an awl, then repeat on the other side.

8 | SCREW IN THE HANGERS
Screw the hanger into the frame at the spots you marked with the awl. Make sure the hanging part is positioned slightly upward.

 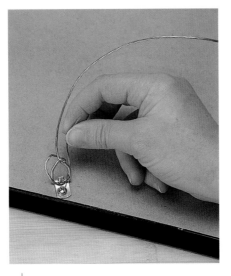 

9 THREAD WIRE THROUGH THE HANGER
Cut a piece of wire about 6" (15cm) longer than the width of the frame. To make a framer's knot, thread the wire through the hanger, from the center of the frame toward the outside. Bring the end of the wire around to the right and under the wire.

10 PULL THE WIRE TIGHT
Thread the wire back through the hanger from the top, going down back toward the center of the frame and pull the wire tight.

11 WRAP THE WIRE END AND TRIM
Twist the tail of the wire around the length of wire 5–7 times and trim.

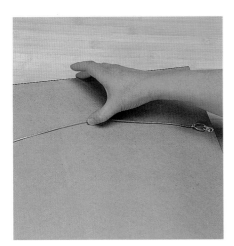 

12 REPEAT FOR THE OTHER SIDE
Repeat on the other hanger, pulling the wire so that it's loose, but not real loose. If you like, place bumpons (self-adhesive felt or rubber circles) on the back of the bottom two corners, to protect the wall.

WIRELESS HANGING

Another way to hang a frame is to attach a sawtooth hanger in the center of the top of the frame. Use your tape measure to find the center, then place the center of the sawtooth at that point. Use a pencil or scratch awl to mark the position, then use nails to attach the hanger.

Traditional Framing Solutions

I don't know about you, but I love variety. I mean, I *really* love variety. I think that was what I loved about Frame Concepts, the last frame shop I worked in. When I was there we had over one thousand molding samples to choose from and, dare I say, even more mat colors. Not only did I always find just the right frame for a client's piece, but I usually had to pick between several "perfect" choices. While not all frame shops are going to have this kind of selection, there is more choice available today than there ever has been before. If you can't find what you need from your local shop, try online. And mat board and molding are not only sold in frame shops; they are available at art and craft supply stores as well. The days of just seeing basic oak, gold and black are over, so be prepared to be "wowed."

The projects in this section are referred to as "traditional" framing solutions, not because of their style per se, but because they use what we are all familiar with as the traditional components of framing: a frame, glass, matting (most of the time) and a wire. Sometimes a ready-made frame is used and sometimes the molding is custom ordered. Knowing that you have the option of using either one offers you more flexibility. We'll explore techniques from mounting three-dimensional objects to cutting multiple openings in a mat to stretching a piece of needlework. As we go along, I'm sure you'll be able to think of many ways you can apply these methods to your own pieces of art.

Decorating a Mat Using a Tape Mask

Mat decoration is an easy way to dress up a project or to give it an instant upgrade. Typically, this approach is used on slightly more formal pieces, but I have decorated mats on projects of all styles. While there are as many ways to decorate a mat as there are ways to add color to paper, this particular mat has been decorated with gold French lines and pastel chalks. When decorating a mat, it is easiest to work with smooth-surfaced mats that have been specially sized to accept ink without bleeding. It never hurts to test a small scrap of the mat with the medium you'd like to try before actually coloring on the mat itself.

While the treatment for this piece is very traditional, pastels may be used in a more contemporary way by adding irregular color to the reveal of a bottom mat. Or jazz up the mat by using a pencil or another color of pen to hand-draw a line around the opening.

WHAT ELSE YOU'LL LEARN

- *How to cut a reverse bevel*
- *How to rule French lines*

WHAT YOU'LL NEED

khaki smooth-surfaced 4-ply mat board

pale peach 4-ply mat board

white crackled mat board

acid-free foam board

joined frame

glass, cut to size

mat cutter

cork-backed ruler

basic tool kit (see page 11)

finishing hardware

fine-point gold paint pen

decorator chalks

pencil

white eraser

adhesive transfer tape

removable tape

artist's tape

acid-free photo corners

kraft paper (for dust cover)

ABOUT THE ARTWORK

I found this vintage botanical at a booth in an antique market. It was framed with no mat in a dark brown, rather boring frame. With its pretty tones of pink and sage green, I immediately saw its potential to be reframed with a decorated mat and a lighter-wood frame. The end result is a shabby-chic treasure.

1 CUT A REVERSE BEVEL FOR THE BOTTOM MAT

For this project I made the top and the middle mat beveled and cut the bottom mat with a reverse bevel. To make a reverse bevel, instead of positioning the cutting head inside of the opening, move the mat to the left so that the head is outside of the opening. Also, instead of cutting beyond the horizontals, start the cut for a reverse bevel with the blade point right on the top horizontal line, and cut until the edge of the blade just reaches the bottom horizontal line.

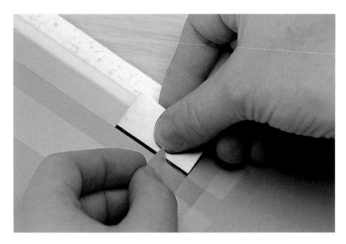

2 LIGHTLY RULE PENCIL LINES

To create a border around the opening of the top mat, measure out an equal distance all around the opening (in this case $7/16$" [11mm]). Make light pencil marks on each side of each corner. Connect the marks with a light pencil line. Measure a distance from the first line to make a second line to form a band (in this case $3/8$" [10mm]). Erase any pencil marks that extend beyond the corners; you won't be able to erase these marks once you've applied the chalks.

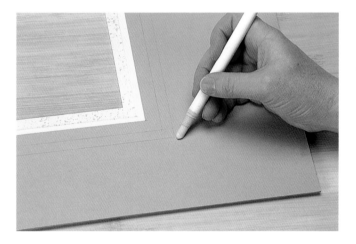

3 TAPE AROUND THE BAND

Place removable tape right on the lines toward the outside of the mat. Then place tape on the lines toward the opening of the mat, leaving the band you will be decorating exposed. To remove tape from inside of the band, place a razor blade along one side of the tape, then pull the perpendicular piece of tape against the razor blade to cut it.

4 ADD COLOR WITH CHALK

Select a chalk color that is present in your artwork and that you think goes nicely with the mat color. Apply the color with your finger or with a cosmetic applicator, concentrating the darkest color in the corners. Work the color in well with your finger to reduce the amount of loose chalk on the mat. If you get any stray chalk marks on the mat, use a white eraser to remove them.

An alternative way to apply the pastels is to scrape powder from the stick with a razor blade onto a scrap of paper. Pick up the color with your finger or an applicator from there.

5 | RULE IN FRENCH LINES
Carefully remove the tape from the border. Using a fine-point paint pen and a cork-backed ruler, outline both sides of the border, creating the inside lines first. To get a feel for the pen, try tracing a line on a piece of scrap paper first.

6 | MOUNT THE ARTWORK
To finish the project, create a hinge along one side of the foam board backing, using artist's tape. Bring the mat up to meet the tape and burnish. Close the mat and make sure it's aligned with the backing, then position the artwork under the mat. Place a weight on the artwork to hold it in place. Apply photo corners around the artwork and burnish them down. You're now ready to clean the glass and fit the artwork into the frame. (See Putting It All Together on page 27.)

CUTTING CLOCKWISE

When cutting a reverse bevel mat, rotate the mat clockwise after the first cut. When you make the second cut, you'll be able to actually feel where the first cut ended and where you should stop. Continue rotating clockwise after each cut.

VARIATION

SPOTTED MAT

Instead of ruling lines onto a mat, try randomly painting shapes (in this case, spots) that are a reflection of the artwork. Here, I used a black watercolor crayon and a water brush. The white bottom mat gives your eye a place to rest between the spots on the mat and the artwork (created by Margaret Hopkins). This prevents the spots from making the overall piece too busy.

Mounting a Textile

Many of us have heirloom textiles such as crocheted doilies, handkerchiefs or even baby clothes that are just sitting forgotten in our hope chests. Why not make them lovely works of art by framing them? Stitching down textiles to a background mat (called a float mat) is easy, especially when the textiles are small.

For pieces that are octagonal, it's fun to cut a mat that is the same shape. An octagonal mat would also work nicely on a piece of artwork that is circular. Not only does this make the piece look more custom, it cuts down on the negative space left outside of the textile, and therefore is less distracting for the piece.

WHAT ELSE YOU'LL LEARN

• *How to cut an octagonal mat*

• *How to prevent fabric mats from fraying*

• *How to add depth with foam board*

ABOUT THE ARTWORK

Because this doily is white, I was free to choose whatever colors I wanted for the mat and frame. Because it is old, I wanted to keep the look traditional, yet still give it just a touch of panache. The distressed frame stays in tune with an antique look, while the richly-textured chenille mat provides plenty of style.

WHAT YOU'LL NEED

chenille mat board

black mat board (or color of your choice)

acid-free foam board

joined frame

glass, cut to size

mat cutter

ruler

basic tool kit (see page 11)

finishing hardware

thread to match textile

needle

T-pin or needle tool

scissors

pencil

adhesive transfer tape

artist's tape

clear-drying craft glue

kraft paper (for dust cover)

1 MAP OUT THE SHAPE OF AN OCTAGON
On the back of the chenille mat board, map out the shape of an octagon according to the size of your textile. See page 41 for assistance on configuring an even-sided octagon.

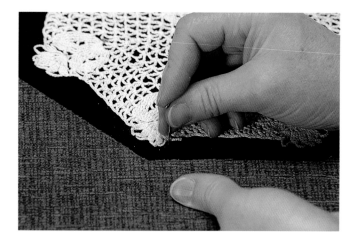

2 CUT ALL EIGHT SIDES
Cut the mat using the same technique as described on page 17. Cut two parallel sides, then rotate the mat 90 degrees and cut the other two parallel sides. Rotate the mat 45 degrees, cut those two parallel sides, then cut the remaining two sides. Don't worry at this point if some of the chenille fibers overhang the mat opening; you'll clean that up later.

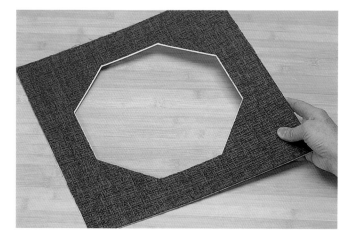

3 TACK THE TEXTILE DOWN WITH THREAD
Place the cut-out mat over the black bottom mat and position the textile in the center. Use a dressmaker's T-pin to poke two holes through the mat at inconspicuous spots at each corner of the textile and in six or eight spots in the center. Select thread the same color as the textile, and thread it on a needle. Push the needle up through one of the holes, then down through the second hole, catching a small piece of the textile with the needle and thread.

4 KNOT THE THREAD AND REPEAT
Slide the mat to the edge of the table and pull both lengths of the thread taut. Knot the thread on the back. Avoid turning the mat over to keep the unstitched portion of the doily in place. Cut the thread above the knot and repeat the process for each set of holes you poked in the mat.

5 SECURE KNOTS WITH TAPE
Turn the mat over so it is facedown, and place strips of artist's tape over the knots.

6 CUT STRIPS FOR THE SIDES
To create some depth between the textile and the window mat, build up the window mat with foam board. To do this, cut strips that are ³/₈" (10mm) narrower than the width of the mat sides, so that they won't be visible from the front. Use adhesive transfer tape to apply the strips to the back of the mat.

7 MEASURE FOR FILL-IN CORNERS
Measure from one corner of the octagon to the corner created by the foam board. Subtract ³/₈" (10mm) from that measurement and cut 2 squares that size. Cut those squares in half diagonally.

8 COMPLETE FOAM BOARD BUILD-UP
Use adhesive transfer tape to attach the four foam board triangles to the inside of the four corners around the mat.

9 CLEAN UP THE BEVEL
Thin a bit of clear-drying craft glue with water. Use this mixture and your finger to clean up the cut edges of the chenille by smoothing down the fibers.

10 SECURE THE MATS TOGETHER
Apply adhesive transfer tape to the back of the foam board. Center the chenille mat over the textile and press down, to adhere it to the bottom mat.

11 CLEAN OFF THE MAT
Check the chenille mat for lint. Remove lint by wrapping your finger in tape and patting over the lint. (This works well on any fabric mat.)

12 FIT THE FINISHED PIECE INTO A FRAME
Cut a piece of foam board backing to go behind the textile mat. Clean the glass, and sandwich it with the art. Secure the glass, artwork and backing into the frame using a point driver. Finish with a dust cover and hanger (see Putting It All Together, page 27).

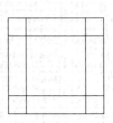

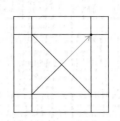

1. *Measure width of textile, then add desired space around it.*

2. *Draw a square in the center for the textile, then add borders for the space around.*

3. *Draw an X inside the square to determine its center, then measure from the center to one corner.*

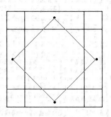

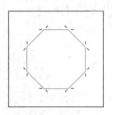

4. *Draw lines the length found in step 3 that radiate from the center of the square and that are parallel to the square sides.*

5. *Connect the ends of the lines measured in step 4 to form a new square.*

6. *Draw in the now visible octagon sides and erase all other lines.*

VARIATION

DIAMOND MATS

Hand-painted ceramic tiles can be framed in the orientation of a diamond, with the mat cut to the same shape. This is another example of floating. Because sewing wasn't an option, silicone was used to secure the tiles to the back mat.

3

Reducing the Size of a Premade Frame

Inevitably you're going to find a frame that you'd love to use but that is too big for your artwork. The solution? Break it apart and cut it down. This is a great way to recycle and cut costs at the same time. Most premade frames are not difficult to break apart and cut down to a smaller, more custom-fit size. Before you go smashing up any frame, however, keep in mind that in breaking apart a frame, a certain amount near the corners is damaged and will not be able to be used. I snagged this frame at a yard sale, but it was too large for the diploma I wanted to frame, so breaking and cutting it down was the perfect solution.

WHAT ELSE YOU'LL LEARN

- *How to decorate a mat board with paper*
- *How to "cheat" with a bottom mat that you thought was too small*

ABOUT THE ARTWORK

I love the look of a black-core mat on any piece of artwork that has a significant amount of black text. It seems to sharpen everything up. Because there wasn't too much in the way of color in the diploma, I was free to find a decorative paper that coordinated nicely with the frame, and I wasn't limited by what was present in the artwork. When framing diplomas or documents, feel free to try decorative papers or other mat decorating strategies to spruce up what might otherwise be a sterile or uninteresting piece of artwork. School colors can be used as an accent in the bottom mat. This is one time when you can really frame to suit the room (such as an office) rather than just the artwork.

WHAT YOU'LL NEED

black-core top mat

black-core bottom mat (will be covered with paper)

decorative paper

acid-free foam board

ready-made frame (to be cut down)

glass, cut to size

mat cutter

iron

basic tool kit (see page 11)

finishing hardware

white pencil (to mark on black mat)

spray adhesive

adhesive transfer tape

artist's tape

acid-free photo corners

kraft paper (for dust cover)

1 | BREAK THE GLUE SEAL
Remove any reinforcement corners and all staples from the back of the frame. To loosen the glue at the corners of the frame, firmly tap each corner down onto the work surface. This seems scary, but use enough force to break the seal.

2 | CAREFULLY PRY THE FRAME APART
Place the frame diagonally on the edge of the work surface, and loosen the frame further by prying it down in each direction.

3 | PULL OUT THE NAILS
Pull the frame completely apart. Find the pieces that have nails and use wire cutters to gently wiggle them out. If you do tear a nail, just be sure to make your cuts away from the nail so that you don't ruin your saw blade. Cut each side down to the new size and rejoin the frame. (See pages 23–26 for more on cutting and joining frames.)

A BETTER BREAKDOWN

Overall, this process of breaking down a frame works better on frames that have been v-nailed (joined with a V-shaped staple that is forced into the back of the frame to hold the mitered corner together), not frames that are hand-nailed from the sides.

4 | MOUNT PAPER ONTO THE BOTTOM MAT
To decorate a mat board with paper, spray the back of the paper with spray adhesive in a well ventilated area. Smooth the paper over what will be the bottom mat board. Note that the decorative paper doesn't need to be as large as the mat board; it just needs to be big enough to cover what will be the mat opening and reveal.

5 | APPLY HEAT TO STRENGTHEN THE BOND
To help the paper adhere even better, run a dry iron (no steam) over the paper. Set the iron on medium heat.

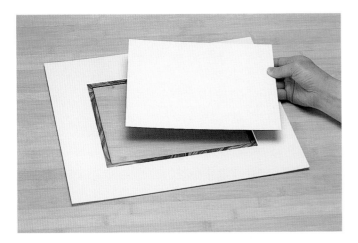

6 CUT THE DOUBLE MAT
Cut the opening in the top mat. Use adhesive transfer tape to adhere the paper-covered mat to the top mat and the fallout (see page 18). Place the mat facedown on the cutter and cut the bottom mat. Turn the mat over and remove the fallout.

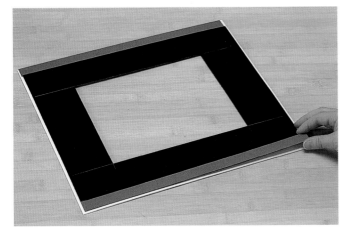

7 FILL IN LARGE GAPS
If your bottom mat board is much smaller than your top, cut strips of scrap mat board to make up the difference. Adhere the strips with adhesive transfer tape. The bottom mat is always a bit smaller than the top mat (see page 18), but if it's a lot smaller, the top mat may bow when it's nailed into the frame.

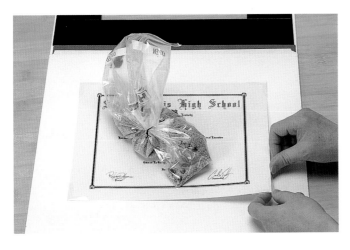

8 SECURE THE ARTWORK TO THE BACKING
Cut a backing board, then hinge it to the mat with artist's tape. Position your document on the foam board backing and weight it down with a bag of sand or rice. Use tape or photo corners to adhere the document to the backing.

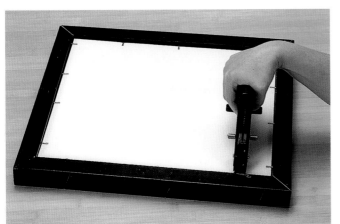

9 FIT EVERYTHING TOGETHER
Clean the glass with glass cleaner and a terrycloth towel. Brush the glass and the matted document, then place everything in the frame. Use a point driver to secure the backing to the frame. To finish the frame, add a dust cover, then secure a wire to the back for hanging (see Putting It All Together, page 27).

Cutting a Multi-Opening Mat

Matting multiple pieces together in one frame is not only a great way to present individual pieces as a complete group, but it's actually more economical than matting and framing each piece separately. When choosing matting for a collection of images, the key is to find common denominators.

An 8-ply mat or double-thick mat, as it's sometimes called, adds depth with a dramatically wider-than-normal bevel. This is one easy way to suggest your piece is special. Combine a white mat with a black frame and you have a tried-and-true solution for nearly any image, especially a collection of black-and-white photos.

WHAT ELSE YOU'LL LEARN

- *How to cut an 8-ply mat*
- *How to make decorative designs in mat board*
- *How to assemble a metal frame*

WHAT YOU'LL NEED

4-ply white rag mat board

8-ply white rag mat board

acid-free foam board

metal frame

metal frame hardware (including hanging hardware)

glass, cut to size

mat cutter

transparent ruler

flat-head screwdriver

wire

pencil

adhesive transfer tape

artist's tape

acid-free photo corners

ABOUT THE ARTWORK

These beautiful photos were taken by Tricia Waddell during her vacation to Italy. When I saw the striking elements of the subject matter, I wanted to create a mat that would reflect an architectural style, but be elegantly understated. The white-on-white effect of the mat worked perfectly.

1 | MAP OUT ALL THE OPENINGS

Use adhesive transfer tape to tape the 8-ply mat board to the 4-ply mat board. Place the tape where you won't be making cuts, around the very edge of the mat in this case. Use just enough tape to hold the boards together, as you will separate them later. Map out the cuts for the images only on the back of the 8-ply mat. Remember to account for the reveal of the top mat when you are deciding on placement and the amount between openings. Use a pencil to circle the intersections of the lines so that it's easy to see where you will need to start and stop when you're cutting.

2 | CUT THE 8-PLY MAT

Position your blade for cutting an 8-ply mat (or adjust the blade so that it is extended twice as far as it usually is for a 4-ply mat). Practice cutting on a scrap piece of 8-ply mat, then cut the openings you've marked. Make your cuts so that they extend about ³/₈" (10mm) beyond the intersection.

WHAT YOUR NUMBERS REVEAL

A good way to remember your measurements is to write them on the back of the mat. This is especially helpful when the top is different than the sides, as well as when there is more than one mat.

3 | RULE LINES FOR MAIN OPENINGS ON THE TOP MAT

Separate the two pieces of mat board, remove the fallout from the double-thick mat and set that mat aside. Use the score lines from cutting the double-thick mat to map out the cuts on the top mat. Here I measured ⁵/₈" (16mm) from the score lines to create a larger opening in the top mat.

4 MAP OUT CREATIVE ELEMENTS

Continue to map out the decorative cutting. Use a transparent ruler to make the pencil marks easier to align. Here I've made 1" (3cm) squares at the corners and used ½"-wide (13mm) bars to connect the squares. Create your own design for whatever looks best for your piece.

5 CUT OUT ALL OF THE OPENINGS

Cut all the openings on the mat, cutting all the lefthand edges first, then the right, and finally the top and bottom.

6 APPLY TAPE TO THE BACK OF THE MAT

Apply adhesive transfer tape around all of the openings on the mat you just cut (the top mat).

7 ADHERE THE TWO MATS TOGETHER

Line up the taped mat on the double-thick mat and press in place. Make sure all areas of the mats are secured with the tape.

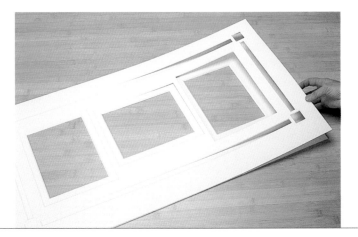

8 MOUNT THE PHOTOS TO THE BACKING
Use artist's tape to hinge the completed mat to the top edge of the foam board backing. Position the photos under the openings. Use photo corners to secure the photos in place.

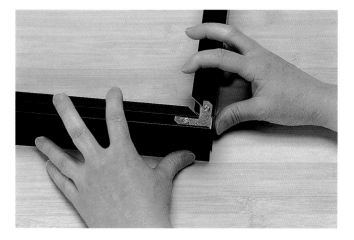

9 LAY OUT THE FRAME RAILS AND HARDWARE
Clean the glass and set it on the artwork. Put it aside. Turn the rails of the frame over and first connect one long side to one short side. There is a flat back plate and a top plate with screws for each corner. Slide the stacked plates into the channel of the first piece and slide the adjacent piece onto the plates.

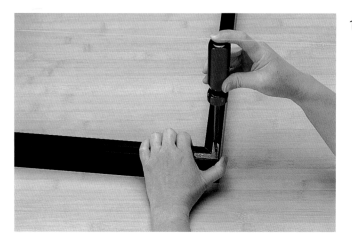

10 TIGHTEN THE FIRST CORNER
Hold the pieces together while you tighten the screws in place.

11 SLIDE IN THE GLASS AND ARTWORK
Join the second long rail to the first short rail. Leave the other short rail off of the frame for now. Turn the frame faceup and slide the glass and artwork into the frame.

FRAME IT!

12 | SLIDE REMAINING PLATES INTO THE RAIL
Turn the frame facedown and insert the last two hardware corners into the short rail.

13 | SLIDE THE RAIL ONTO THE REST OF THE FRAME
Insert the plates of both corners simultaneously into the two long rails.

14 | ADD SPRING CLIPS
Tighten these screws, then go back and tighten the other corners if necessary. Insert spring clips on all four sides of the frame, placing them about 2" (5cm) apart (putting them closer together may put too much pressure on the glass). If needed, bend the spring clips slightly to loosen them so that you can slide them under the channel of the frame.

15 | ADD THE HANGING HARDWARE AND WIRE
Clip the hangers onto the channel, placing them about one-third of the way down the frame. Screw the hangers to tighten them, then attach wire as described on page 29.

Creating a Folded-Side Shadow Box

A folded-side shadow box is a quick way to create a box of any desired depth for your artwork. This method is easy, and it saves you time by eliminating the need to first mount a piece of mat board to foam board and then measure and cut strips. In addition, the result is a seamless look.

The individual boxes behind these five openings remind me of little dioramas, each one telling a different story. Consider making each box a different color or texture. You could also mount decorative paper to a mat board before cutting and scoring it, to provide contrast to a neutral top mat.

Ready-made shadow box frames are getting easier to come by. This frame came with a strip of velcro and a black fabric interior, neither of which I needed, but I did appreciate its depth and elongated shape.

WHAT ELSE YOU'LL LEARN

- *How to cut a multi-opening mat*
- *How to adapt a ready-made shadow box frame*

ABOUT THE ARTWORK

As a collector of manual typewriters, I wanted to create a piece that expressed what I truly love—type! I thought it would be fun to try and create "original" font designs for these individual typesetting pieces. After sketching out the letters in pencil, on regular graph paper, I stained the paper in black tea and then ironed them when they were dry. The pieces look genuinely old and have interesting textures and stains.

I wanted a white mat with borders that were dramatically larger than the opening sizes. This makes it very easy for the eye to zoom in on and read the artwork as a whole.

WHAT YOU'LL NEED

white 4-ply mat board

slate blue suede mat board

mat board (for backing)

acid-free foam board

joined frame (ready-made shadow box is ideal)

glass, cut to size

mat cutter

drill

basic tool kit (see page 11)

finishing hardware

screws (for attaching type pieces)

pencil

adhesive transfer tape

artist's tape

craft glue

kraft paper (for dust cover)

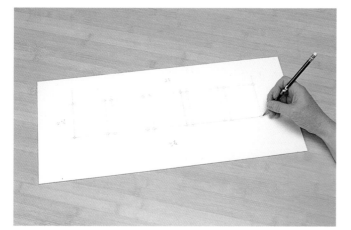 

1 DETERMINE THE MAT OPENING LAYOUT
Cut the mat board to the size of the frame. This ready-made frame was 9" x 20" (23cm x 51cm). I needed five openings, but they could be of any size. I knew that I wanted approximately a 2½" (6cm) top with a weighted bottom. So I determined that my box sizes would each be 3" (8cm) tall. I wanted the mat sides to be slightly wider than the top and I wanted ½" (13mm) between each of the boxes. So to figure the width of the boxes, I used this equation: $20 - (2\frac{3}{4} \times 2) - (\frac{1}{2} \times 4) \div 5 = 2\frac{1}{2}$.

To map this out on the back of the mat board, draw the border around the group of boxes first. Then divide the center area into each of the five boxes. Draw a circle at each corner of each box so that you can easily see where to stop and start the cuts.

2 CUT OUT THE OPENINGS
Use a mat cutter to cut the openings. Cut the top of each opening first, then the bottoms, the left sides and finally the right sides.

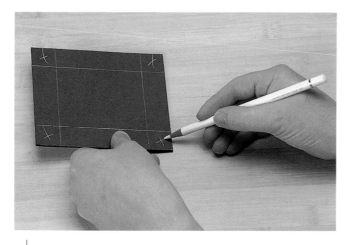 

3 DRAW LINES FOR THE BOX
Determine the size of the suede mat used to make each mini box by referring to the diagram on page 57. The sides of the box should be as tall as the items you're putting in them. With a contrasting pencil, make lines the width of each side.

MAKING THE CUT

If you don't cut all the way through the mat, turn the mat over to the front and use a thin razor blade or mat cutting blade to cut the remaining mat.

4 SCORE THE BOX SIDES

Score the lines using a beveled cut, pushing only lightly so that you don't cut through the mat board. More than one swipe may be needed. Once the line is scored, make a cut through the mat board from the edge of the square to the first intersection of lines. Repeat this for each side to score the lines and cut through to remove the corner pieces.

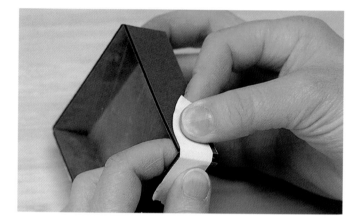

5 FOLD THE BOX SIDES

Fold up the sides of the boxes and secure with artist's tape. Make sure the top edges are aligned before securing with tape. By scoring the mat board on a beveled angle, the corners of the box come together tightly and the beveled edges supply a flat surface for the tape.

6 DRILL A HOLE THROUGH THE PAPER AND THE MAT

Position the paper in the shadow box. Use an $\frac{1}{8}$" (3mm) drill bit (or one large enough to accommodate the screws you'll use to secure the pieces) to drill a hole where you'll place the type piece.

7 DRILL A HOLE IN THE WOODEN TYPE PIECE

Use the same size bit to drill a hole into the type piece.

8 SECURE THE PIECES
Place the screw up through the bottom of the box, and place the type piece over the screw. Use a screwdriver to tighten the screw, holding the type piece in place. As you get close to getting it fully tightened, be sure to straighten the paper and the type piece to your satisfaction.

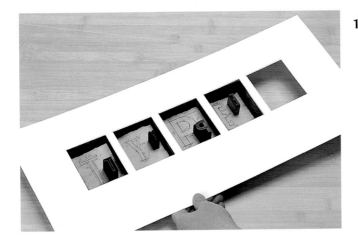

9 APPLY TAPE TO THE BACK OF THE MAT
Place adhesive transfer tape around the openings on the mat board, placing the tape as close as possible to the opening without the tape showing.

10 CENTER BOXES UNDER WINDOWS
Center a box under one of the mat openings. Press to lightly secure, then turn the board over to make sure the back of the box looks square. When it's positioned straight, press firmly. Repeat for each of the boxes.

11 SECURE THE BOXES WITH GLUE
To secure the boxes further, spread craft glue around the outside edges of the boxes. If you can't reach between the boxes with the glue, apply some glue in between with a scrap piece of mat board. Don't apply so much glue that it seeps under the edges of the boxes. Allow to dry completely.

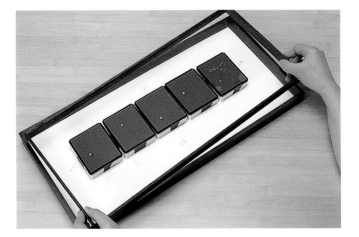

12 | INSERT THE ARTWORK INTO THE FRAME
Clean the glass that comes with the shadow box frame using glass cleaner and a terrycloth towel. Brush off the glass and the matted artwork. Remove the flexible points from the ready-made frame. Place the artwork in the shadow box, on top of the glass. If your ready-made frame comes with an insert, place that over the mat to keep the glass and mat in place.

13 | SUPPORT THE ARTWORK WITH FOAM BOARD
Cut two strips of ⅛" (3mm) foam board the width of the insert. Place a line of craft glue along one thin edge of the foam board. Place the foam board halfway between the insert and the bottom of the mini shadow boxes. Cut and glue another piece and place it between the insert and the top of the boxes. Measure the distance between your two foam board strips, and cut two more pieces of foam board. Place these on each side of the mini shadow boxes. If your ready-made frame doesn't come with an insert, place foam board around the edges of the frame as well.

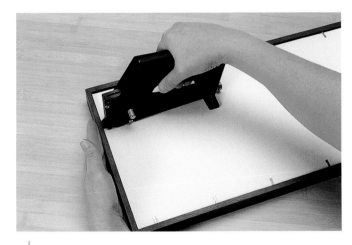

14 | NAIL THE PIECE INTO THE FRAME
Cut a piece of mat board to the size of your frame. Use the point driver to secure everything into the frame. Add a kraft paper dust cover and hanging hardware and wire to finish (see Putting It All Together, page 27).

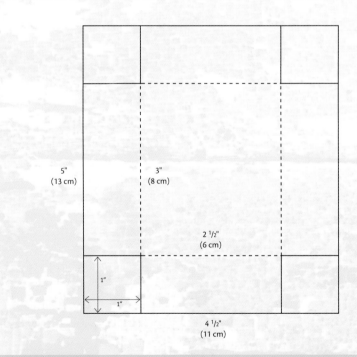

Follow the above diagram to create the 3" x 2½" x ½" (8cm x 6cm x 13mm) mini shadow boxes used in this project.

Wrapping a Mat with Fabric

Wrapping a mat with fabric is an easy way to bring texture to your framing project. While the artwork here happens to use fabric as a medium, fabric-wrapped mats need not be limited to needlepoint or textile work. Fabric left over from another décor project could be used to spruce up a school portrait that hangs in the same room, or consider the elegance of dyed silk on a traditional Asian watercolor. With fabric, your options are as numerous as they would be with paper.

WHAT ELSE YOU'LL LEARN

- *How to stretch and pin needlework*
- *How to decorate a mat with watercolors and colored pencils*
- *How to cut a mat with multiple openings*

ABOUT THE ARTWORK

These whimsical embroidered works are the result of a creative collaboration between sisters Jenny and Christine Doyle. Jenny creates the illustrations for the pieces, while Christine turns them into embroidered textiles. One element that I instantly saw they all had in common was the googly-eyed expressions. I wanted to carry this out into the design of the framing by decorating the mat with fun circles of color that complemented each individual piece. Using a neutral top mat and customizing each opening ties this piece together and can be used anytime you frame with multiple openings.

I tried laying the pieces out horizontally at first, but after trying them vertically, I decided the group was easier to read top to bottom.

WHAT YOU'LL NEED

neutral mat board (which will be covered with fabric)

white 4-ply mat board

lightweight fabric (enough to cover the top mat)

acid-free foam board

joined frame

glass, cut to size

mat cutter

iron

ruler

craft knife

cutting mat

silk pins or dressmaker's pins

water brush or small paintbrush

basic tool kit (see page 11)

finishing hardware

watercolor crayons

colored pencils

pencil

artist's tape

adhesive transfer tape

spray adhesive

kraft paper (for dust cover)

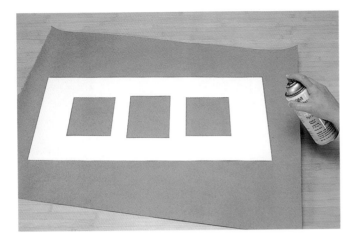

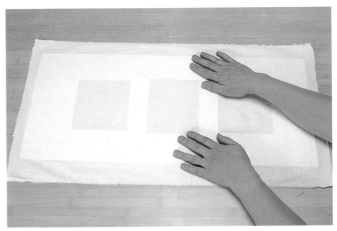

1 | CUT THE TOP MAT AND SPRAY WITH ADHESIVE
Measure your needlework, and cut the openings in the neutral top mat. To show off the decorating that you'll start in step 12, plan on including ⅜"–⅝" (10mm–16mm) for a reveal when configuring your opening sizes. Use a reverse bevel cut for this top mat, or cut using a regular bevel and plan to wrap the fabric around the reverse side. Spray the front of the mat with spray adhesive in a well-ventilated area.

2 | ADHERE FABRIC TO THE TOP MAT
Lay the fabric down over the sticky mat and smooth it out. Position the fabric so the grain is square with the openings in the mat. If the fabric goes down crooked, peel it up and reposition it.

3 | APPLY HEAT TO THE FABRIC
Using a dry iron (no steam), apply heat to the mounted fabric to strengthen the bond.

4 | APPLY TAPE TO THE FIRST EDGE
Turn the mat over and trim any excess fabric, leaving 1" (3cm) of overhang on all sides. Cut squares out of the corners to make folding them easier. Place one piece of adhesive transfer tape down so that it lays on both the mat and the fabric. Burnish the tape down over the edge of the board with your fingernail.

5 | SECURE THE FABRIC EDGE DOWN
Remove the backing from the tape. Use your thumb to burnish the fabric to the mat, working from one end to the other. Be sure the fabric is adhered firmly to the edge of the mat, as well as to the front and back. Overlap the fabric in the corners.

6 | REMOVE EXCESS FROM OPENINGS
Use a craft knife or fabric scissors to cut the excess fabric from the centers of the mat openings. Cut out the centers, leaving ¹/₂" (13mm) of overhang around the edges of each opening.

7 | CUT SLITS IN THE CORNERS
Tape around one opening, placing the tape on both the mat and the fabric as you did in step 4. Burnish the tape onto the bevel with your fingernail. Remove the backing of the tape, then place the mat on a cutting board. Place the tip of your craft knife blade two threads away from the corner, and make a slit in the fabric. Repeat for each of the corners in that opening.

8 | BURNISH TO MAKE A SHARP CORNER
Wrap the fabric around the edge of the opening, using your thumbnail to secure the fabric into the corner. Burnish the fabric to the mat with your fingers.

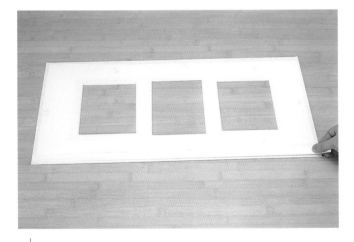

9 | PROTECT FABRIC EDGES WITH TAPE
Repeat steps 7 and 8 for each of the remaining openings. With artist's tape, secure all the edges of the fabric to the back of the mat.

10 | TRACE OPENINGS ONTO THE BOTTOM MAT
Place the fabric-wrapped mat face down onto the bottom mat. Lightly trace the shape of the openings onto the bottom mat, being careful not to get pencil marks on the fabric.

11 ADD COLORED PENCIL CIRCLES

Remove the top mat and draw light guidelines ³⁄₈" (10mm) to the inside of the first lines, taking care not to draw the lines all the way to the corners. Make your mat decorations between the two lines, extending the decoration about ¹⁄₈" (3mm) past the outer line. Here I began the decorations by using a circle template and a colored pencil to make orange circles around the opening. Take care to stagger the circles so that some cross the lines and others are in between the lines.

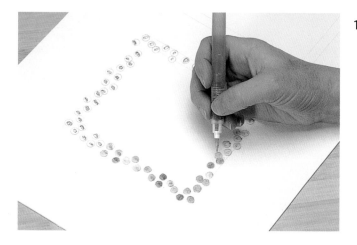

12 APPLY WATERCOLOR

To finish the decorations, color the circles in with watercolor crayons. Then use a water brush to wet the crayon and make the circles look painted.

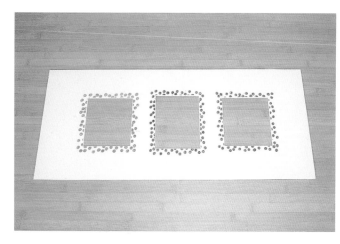

13 CUT OPENINGS IN THE DECORATED MAT

Repeat around the other openings. Here I used blue, green and tan watercolor crayons to color the circles because they matched the thread colors in the embroidery pieces. Once the water has dried, go back with the orange colored pencil and freehand the circles around the colors. To cut the bottom mat, turn the mat over and trace the top mat openings onto the back. Measure in ¹⁄₄" (6mm) from the line and cut along this line with the mat cutter.

14 BEGIN PINNING NEEDLEWORK

Apply adhesive transfer tape to the back of the top mat and adhere it to the bottom mat. Cut pieces of foam board that are slightly larger than the bottom mat's openings. To pin the fabric to the board, center the fabric over the board, fold the fabric over the edge, then insert a pin halfway into the edge of the foam board at the center of the image.

15 | COMPLETE THE PINNING

Pull the fabric (not supertight) and insert a pin on the opposite side. Then turn the board and insert pins in the remaining two sides. Continue to insert pins in alternating sides of the board until the fabric is taut and smooth. Make sure the grain of the fabric remains straight with the edge of the board. For this fabric I placed pins approximately ³/₈" (10mm) apart; the distance depends on the design of the artwork and the fabric it's on.

16 | SECURE FABRIC TO THE BACK

Use a hammer to gently tap the pins into the board. Repeat for each of the pieces of fabric. If you like, trim the edges of the fabric, leaving approximately 1" (3cm) of overhang. Cut out the corners as you did in step 4. Place artist's tape on the fabric overhang and secure it to the back of the foam board, pulling the fabric taut to reduce the bulk. Repeat for each side and each piece of artwork.

17 | FILL IN WITH FOAM BOARD

Center the pinned pieces behind the openings. To build up the mat, cut pieces of foam board to fit between the edges of the mat and the pieces of artwork. Cut the foam board so that the pieces fit snugly together, and adhere the strips to the mat using adhesive transfer tape.

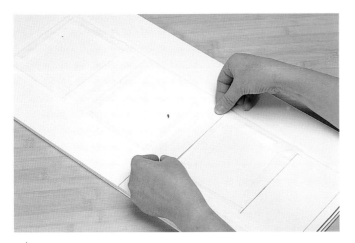 

18 | SECURE THE PINNED PIECES

If you don't mind putting tape on the back of the needlework fabric, use artist's tape to secure the artwork to the foam board strips. If you prefer not to tape the fabric, cut a piece of mat board to the size of the artwork and place it over the back of the artwork. Then adhere the mat board to the foam board strips with adhesive transfer tape.

19 | FIT THE ARTWORK INTO THE FRAME

To finish the piece, clean the glass, place the glass and the artwork into the frame and use a point driver to secure the foam board to the frame. Tape kraft paper over the back and secure a wire on the back to hang. (See Putting It All Together, page 27.)

Cutting Decorative Mat Corners

Decorative corners are one way to repeat a motif or style that is present in your artwork, and they add instant panache to your finished project. The fancy corners that you'll learn to cut in this project look difficult, but they definitely are not. Photos from a bygone era often were mounted on decorative boards that were highly ornate. These mat corners continue that effect. Use your imagination and experiment with different designs of your own. The key to any design is careful measuring and mindful cutting.

This project works with two photos, but you might consider framing several photos together, giving different corner treatments to each. These decorative corners work just as well directly on top of the images, without the float mat shown here.

WHAT ELSE YOU'LL LEARN

- *How to cut a multi-opening mat*
- *How to add depth with foam board*

ABOUT THE ARTWORK

How often have you looked at a photo of someone that was taken long ago and wondered who they were? I thought it would be fun to add labels containing the names and ages of the subjects to give the viewer at least a smidgen of information.

I loved these antique cast paper photo frames and didn't want to cover them up. So I made them a stage for the photos by floating them on a mat and cutting decorative corners in each mat opening that surrounds them.

WHAT YOU'LL NEED

three colors of 4-ply mat board (to suit your artwork)

acid-free foam board

joined frame

glass, cut to size

mat cutter

ruler

basic tool kit (see page 11)

finishing hardware

walnut ink or tea

decorative brads

pencil

adhesive transfer tape

archival craft glue

kraft paper (for dust cover)

1 | MAP OUT THE TOP MAT
Cut your mat boards to size. (All three can be the same size.) On the top mat, map out your two decorative-corner openings, following the illustration below to draw in the corners.

2 | CUT OUT THE TWO OPENINGS
Cut out the openings in the top mat. Make sure to follow the corner cuts carefully, always keeping your cutter on the inner side of the opening.

3 | TRACE THE OPENINGS
Set the mat you just cut facedown on the back of the second mat. Trace the straight edges of the cut opening lightly with a pencil. Do not trace the corners.

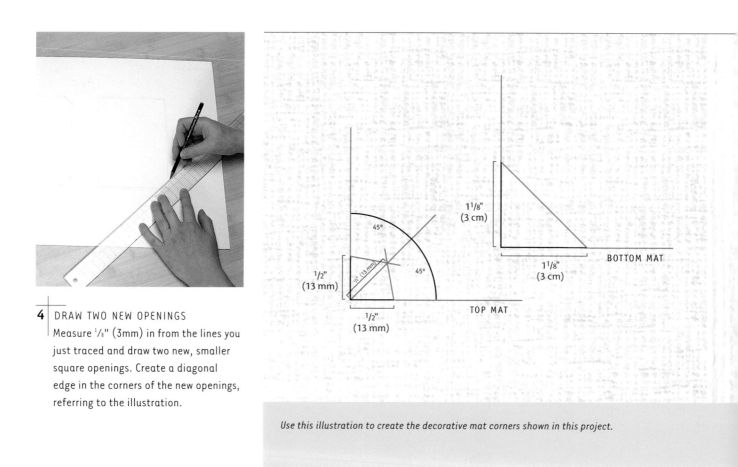

4 | DRAW TWO NEW OPENINGS
Measure ¹/₈" (3mm) in from the lines you just traced and draw two new, smaller square openings. Create a diagonal edge in the corners of the new openings, referring to the illustration.

45°

45°

¹/₂"
(13 mm)

¹/₈ (13 mm)

¹/₂"
(13 mm)

TOP MAT

1¹/₈"
(3 cm)

1¹/₈"
(3 cm)

BOTTOM MAT

Use this illustration to create the decorative mat corners shown in this project.

5 | CUT THE BOTTOM MAT
Cut out the openings in the bottom mat. Make sure you are cutting on the newly drawn, inner lines, and not the traced ones.

6 | BUILD UP THE MAT
Use adhesive transfer tape to adhere the top mat to the bottom mat, carefully positioning the openings. Because my images for this piece are slightly raised, I built up the mat. To do this, cut foam board 1/4" (6mm) narrower than the width of the borders around the openings. Tape the foam board to the back of the mat using adhesive transfer tape, lining up the edges of the foam board with the outside edges of the mat. Cut a piece of foam board to fit between the mat openings, and tape the piece between the openings.

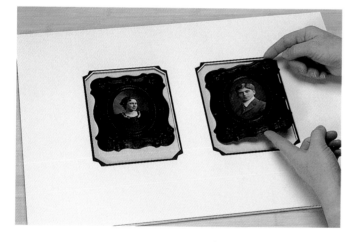

7 | SECURE IMAGES ONTO BACK MAT
Place adhesive transfer tape on the foam board and adhere the mat to the float mat. Adhere your artwork to the float mat. Here I used craft glue to adhere these cardboard frames.

8 | ADD THE LABELS TO FINISH
To make the labels, I printed the words on my computer and stained the paper with walnut ink (or you could use tea). Insert brads into the ends of the labels, spread the flanges and use a hammer to flatten them. Tape the labels to the float mat, centered below the images. Fit the glass and artwork into the frame using the point driver, and finish with kraft paper and hanging hardware (see Putting It All Together, page 27).

8

Adapting a Ready-Made Frame to Be a Shadow Box

Don't let a little thing like available depth stop you from putting a frame you love on a highly dimensional object. You can easily get around the challenge by mounting strips of mat board to extend beyond the back of the frame. Offset clips keep everything securely in the frame, and the viewer of your finished piece will be none the wiser that you cheated the system!

Consider using this solution for framing any number of dimensional embellishments or mementos. Fishing lures, game pieces, champagne corks and numerous other items have been known to sneak into my framing projects, and more often than not, I haven't used what is officially considered a shadow box frame.

WHAT ELSE YOU'LL LEARN

- *How to cut a fillet*
- *How to cut a reverse bevel*
- *How to secure dimensional items with wire*

ABOUT THE ARTWORK

Don't you just love flatware as art? I guess it appeals to my passion for food, but I love the tarnished color of these spoons as much as I love knowing they had once been functional eating tools. I chose three distinctly different sizes for design interest, and I picked a fillet that I thought would really enhance the warm silver tones of the tarnished silver.

The contrast between the finery of the silver matted in suede and the rustic look of barnwood really appealed to me, but these spoons would have looked just as great in a refined silver frame. Since the store where I bought this frame didn't carry shadow box frames made from the same wood, I simply adapted the shallow depth of it to suit my project.

WHAT YOU'LL NEED

cool gray suede mat board
purple suede mat board
neutral linen mat board
acid-free foam board
joined frame (ready-made is ideal)
antique silver fillet
glass, cut to size
basic tool kit (see page 11)
mat cutter
miter box and saw
hand drill or screwdriver

needle-nose pliers
galvanized wire
ruler
finishing hardware
offset clips (with screws)
pencil
adhesive transfer tape
artist's tape
craft glue
kraft paper (for dust cover)

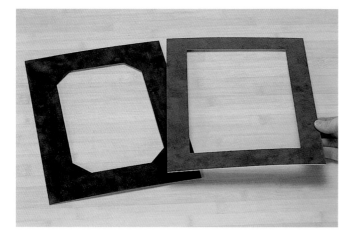

1 | CUT A REVERSE-BEVEL DOUBLE MAT
Cut the openings in your top and bottom mats as desired. Here I made a notched corner in the bottom mat (see diagram on page 73). In this project I used suede mats for both the top and the bottom, and I cut each with a reverse bevel. You'll need to cut a reverse bevel any time you plan on using a fillet. I cut the bottom mat with a reverse bevel also, so that I wouldn't have a white border around the image. (For more on cutting a reverse bevel, see page 34.)

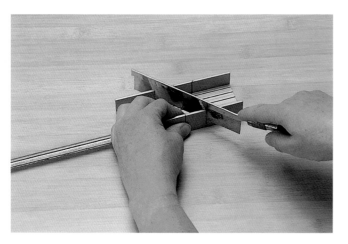

2 | MAKE THE FIRST CUT ON THE FILLET
Make the first 45 degree cut on the fillet, using a saw and a miter box.

3 | MAKE A MARK FOR THE SECOND CUT
Place the piece of fillet along one of the long sides of the top mat opening. Use a pencil to mark where to make your next cut.

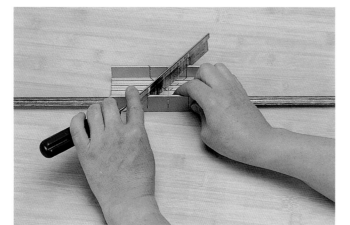

4 | POSITION FILLET AND MAKE THE SECOND CUT
Place the fillet in the miter box so that the angle of the second cut is going in the opposite direction of the first cut. Position the fillet in the box so that the blade will cut through the center of the pencil mark.

FRAME IT!

TERM TO KNOW:
Fillet

This is a special type of molding that is designed to go around the edge of a mat. Available in many colors and styles to coordinate with your frame and artwork, fillet molding comes with a flat ledge to adhere it to the back of the mat. Typically, the fillet will act as a frame for a window mat, but as you will see in Framing Solution 9, it can also work as an outside border for an item that is mounted to mat board and then floated on another mat.

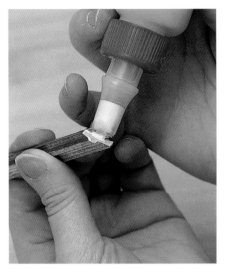

5 ADHERE THE FIRST RAIL TO THE MAT OPENING

Repeat for each of the remaining three sides of the mat. Measure each as you did in step 3 to ensure a good fit. Turn the mat over and place adhesive transfer tape around the back of the opening, as close to the bevel as possible. Turn the mat to the front and position one of the long fillet rails into a corner of the long side. Starting at one end, press down to secure the fillet to the tape on the back and work toward the other corner.

6 APPLY GLUE TO ONE SHORT RAIL

Repeat for the second long side. Place a tiny dab of glue on each cut end of the first short rail.

7 ADHERE SHORT RAILS TO THE MAT OPENING

Position this piece on one short side, then repeat for the second short side.

8 FILL IN THE MAT SPACE

Build up the back of the mat with foam board to the same height as the fillet. To do this, use adhesive transfer tape to adhere the foam board to the mat.

LONG SIDE FIRST

When cutting your fillet, start with the longest sides of the opening. That way if you happen to make a mistake in your cutting, you can reuse the piece for one of the short sides.

9 | PUNCH HOLES TO ADHERE ITEMS
Place adhesive transfer tape on the foam board and attach the top mat to the bottom mat. Set the mats on the float mat (the neutral linen mat) and determine the positioning of the items to be mounted. Use an awl to mark sets of holes through which you'll thread wire to attach the items. Place these holes in inconspicuous areas, if possible.

10 | SEW ITEMS ON WITH WIRE
Set the window mats aside. Use the awl to poke the holes for one item all the way through the float mat. Cut 3" (8cm) lengths of wire, one for each set of holes. Position the first spoon in place. Thread a wire up through one hole from the back, over the spoon and back down through the other hole.

11 | TWIST WIRE IN THE BACK
Turn the float mat over and use needle-nose pliers to twist the wires to secure the spoon to the back. Use wire cutters to trim the wires, then repeat for the remaining spoons. Place artist's tape over the trimmed wire before assembling the frame completely.

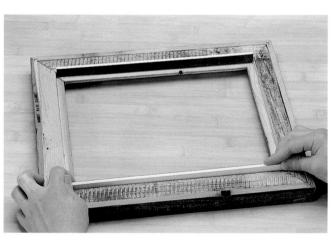

12 | DETERMINE MAT STRIP HEIGHT
Apply adhesive transfer tape to the back of the matted piece and attach it to the front of the float mat. Determine the height needed for the shadow-box strips by placing a scrap of foam board over and perpendicular to the top mat. With a pencil, mark the scrap at the highest point of the stitched-down items. Measure from the bottom of the scrap to the mark. This will be the width of your strips.

13 | ADHERE STRIPS TO THE LONG SIDES OF THE FRAME
Mount a piece of the top mat board to ⅛" (3mm) foam board. Cut four strips that are the width you measured from the last step. Cut two strips to the length of the frame. Clean and set your glass into the frame. Adhere the two long strips to the sides of the frame, using craft or wood glue. It's alright if the strip is taller than the depth of the frame.

14 | CUT AND GLUE IN THE SHORT SIDE STRIPS

To determine the length of the short sides, measure the distance between the long pieces of mat and foam board. Cut two strips to this length and adhere to the frame sides, again using glue.

15 | FIT ARTWORK INTO FRAME WITH OFFSET CLIPS

Brush the glass and your artwork (use artist's tape to remove lint if you're using a suede mat). Place the artwork into the frame, on top of the strips. Use offset clips (available at home improvement, frame shops and hardware stores) to secure the art to the frame. These clips come in a variety of sizes, so choose the one that best fits the height of your piece. Use a screwdriver and screw to secure each clip to the frame. Place the offset clips 2"–3" (5cm–8cm) apart around the frame.

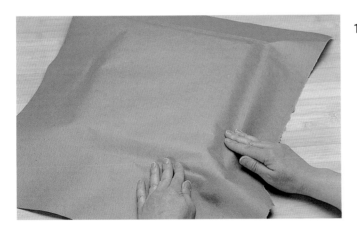

16 | COVER BACK TO FINISH

To finish the back, cut a piece of kraft paper slightly larger than the frame. Place adhesive transfer tape along the edge of the back of the frame. Place the paper over the back of the frame. Gently press the paper onto the center of each side, then run your hands along two sides toward a corner to smooth.

At each corner, crease the paper and fold over any excess. Finally, trim the paper with a razor blade and secure a wire. (See Putting It All Together, page 27.)

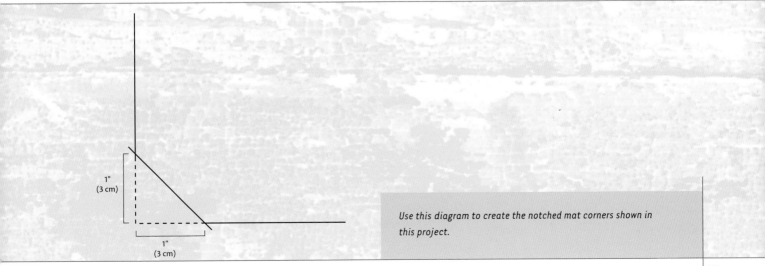

1"
(3 cm)

1"
(3 cm)

Use this diagram to create the notched mat corners shown in this project.

Using a Fillet as a Frame

Some things deserve to be shown off just a bit more than usual, like a wedding invitation, a cherished letter or, in this case, a moment caught in time in the shape of a scrapbook page. While fillets are traditionally cut to trim the window of a mat, they can also be cut with the miter facing the opposite direction to go around the outside of a mounted image.

This solution packs a lot of punch when combined with other three-dimensional objects. The mementos add interest and the fillet further defines the page that is telling the story. Look for a fillet to match your intended frame. Oftentimes a particular molding is designed as part of a larger line that includes a fillet.

WHAT ELSE YOU'LL LEARN

- *How to cut strips for shadow box sides*
- *How to secure dimensional items with glue*

WHAT YOU'LL NEED

light gray 4-ply mat board (speckled)

self-stick or quick mount mat board

acid-free foam board

joined frame

fillet to match frame

glass, cut to size

mat cutter or straightedge and craft knife

basic tool kit (see page 11)

finishing hardware

adhesive transfer tape

archival craft glue

kraft paper (for dust cover)

ABOUT THE ARTWORK

Hope's mother, Marissa Bowers, created this adorable scrapbook page for her, which included the items used as props in the photo taken by Jodi Moran of A Child's Studio. The contrast between the black-and-white photo and the bright, cheerful colors is very dramatic and really draws the viewer into the scene.

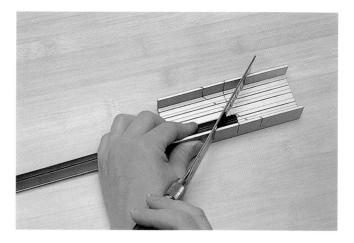

1 CUT THE FILLET
Adhere the scrapbook page to a piece of peel-and-stick mat board of the same size. Cut the fillet so that it will fit around the edges of the mounted page. To do this, miter the corners in the direction so that the flat, ledge portion of the fillet will adhere to the underside of the mounted page.

2 ATTACH THE FILLET TO THE ARTWORK
If you like, use a marker the color of the fillet to color in the cut edges. Adhere the pieces of fillet to the artwork using adhesive transfer tape on the back of the mounted page and craft or wood glue in the corners of the fillet (see steps 2-7 on pages 70-71).

3 FILL IN THE SPACE WITH FOAM BOARD
After all four sides of the fillet are in place, cut a piece of foam board to fit on the back of the artwork, inside of the fillet. To adhere this, place adhesive transfer tape and craft glue on the foam board and press to secure. Here I used artist's tape to piece together two scraps of foam board to create a larger piece.

4 GLUE IN ALL OF THE ELEMENTS
Position the elements on the float mat. To secure the elements, use both adhesive transfer tape and glue. Here I placed the scrapbook page first, then the blocks. To secure the letter P block, I put glue on both the bottom corners of the block and on the scrapbook page. To attach the silk flower, I cut the stem off the flower, leaving 1/4" (6mm) of stem attached to the flower. I punched a hole in the float mat and pushed the cut flower stem through the hole. Then I glued the long portion of the stem to the front of the mat board.

FRAME IT!

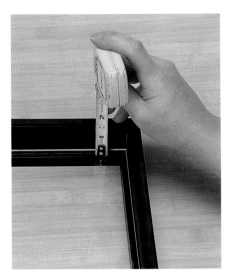

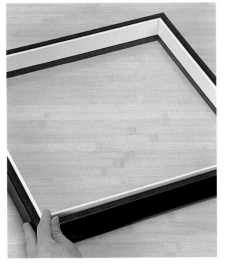

5 | MEASURE FOR SHADOW BOX SIDES
Clean the glass with glass cleaner and a terrycloth towel. Brush off the glass, and insert it into the frame. To determine the height of your shadow box sides, measure the depth of the inside of the frame with the glass in it, then subtract $^{3}/_{16}$" (5mm) (for the depth of the float mat and the foam board that will be placed behind the artwork in step 7).

6 | SECURE STRIPS INTO THE FRAME
Mount scraps of the mat board used for the float mat to foam board and cut strips the width obtained in step 5. Measure the long sides of the frame and cut two strips to this length. Secure the foam board strips to the inside of the frame with adhesive transfer tape and craft glue. Measure the space between the two strips in the frame, and cut the other two mounted strips to that length. Adhere them to the frame sides with more glue and tape.

7 | FIT THE ARTWORK INTO THE FRAME
Dust off the artwork, then insert it into the frame. Cut a piece of foam board to fit the back of the frame and place it over the float mat. Use a point driver to secure everything into the frame. In this case, my foam board was a bit higher than the edge of the frame. If this happens, drive the points in at an angle, then use a hammer to pound them flat, or use offset clips (see step 15, page 73). To finish the back, attach kraft paper and a wire hanger (see Putting It All Together, page 27).

VARIATION

SCRAPBOOK PAGE WITH A WINDOW MAT

STICK-TO-ITIVENESS

When assembling anything in a shadow box, always use some glue in addition to your adhesive transfer tape. Over time the transfer tape can weaken and the items may fall off, but the glue will hold much longer and stay stronger.

The embellishments on this scrapbook page did not require the depth of a shadow box. The window mat was simply raised with one layer of acid-free foam board. Another way to add interest is to add scrapbooking stickers to your mat to give your piece a title.

10

Mounting Collectibles

Collections stored in a box are fine, but why not display them creatively in a shadow box, where you (and everyone else) can enjoy them? This project focuses on baseball cards and a treasured mitt, but any collection of items has framing potential.

If your collectibles aren't as dimensional as this mitt, you might not even need a shadow box. Stamps, concert tickets or score cards are all examples of items that can be displayed together in one frame, without the need for shadow box strips. Custom-made photo corners, like the ones used here, can protect your paper items and visually pull a project together.

WHAT ELSE YOU'LL LEARN

- *How to assemble a stacked shadow box*
- *How to make your own photo corners*
- *How to frame trading cards*
- *How to secure a dimensional object with a nut and bolt*
- *How to cut a mat freehand*
- *How to cut strips for shadow box sides*

WHAT YOU'LL NEED

4-ply mat boards in two team colors

acid-free foam board

shadow box system (Framerica Boxers) cap and 2¼" (6cm) rabbet

glass, cut to size

mat cutter

handheld mat cutter with pointed blade

hand drill or Japanese hole punch

nut and bolt

basic tool kit (see page 11)

ruler

scissors

bone folder

finishing hardware

pencil

adhesive transfer tape

craft glue

wood glue

kraft paper (for dust cover)

ABOUT THE ARTWORK

I still consider Seattle my home, and the Mariners are a part of that home. At the time these cards were published, the colors were blue and gold, so that was the scheme I went with. I could have framed the cards by themselves, but I really wanted to add some dimension and interest, so I added the mitt.

1 ASSEMBLE THE FRAME TOP AND SIDES
This frame is a modular one in which the top and bottom pieces are purchased separately, so that you can get the exact depth and top that you want. To assemble, glue together the pieces of the top and the four sides. Nail the sides to further secure. Place wood glue on the top ledge of the shadow box and place the top part over it.

2 NAIL THE FRAME TOP TO THE SIDES
Mark a hole at each corner of the top of the frame with an awl. Use a drill to start the nail hole, and angle the hole so that the nail will go into the side piece below. Hammer the nail in, then use the nail set to countersink the nail. Fill in the nail hole with wood putty.

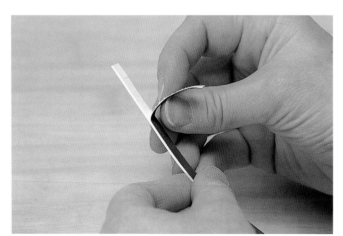

3 CUT MATS FOR THE CARDS
Cut small mat frames for the baseball cards. Then cut a float piece of mat board slightly smaller than the mat frame. Glue the frame to the float mat with craft glue.

4 PEEL PAPER FOR PHOTO CORNERS
To make your own photo corners, cut a piece of mat board to the desired width of the photo corners, in this case ¼" (6mm). Carefully tear the colored paper away from the rest of the mat board, using your fingernail or a craft knife to loosen the end.

5 FOLD ONE SIDE OF THE STRIP
Make a right angle fold with the strip of paper, about 1" (3cm) from the end of the strip.

6 FOLD THE OTHER SIDE
Bring down the other end of the strip to make a triangle, or arrow shape.

7 TRIM THE EXCESS PAPER
Burnish the folds down with a bone folder, then use scissors to trim the ends from the corner. Make a total of four of these for each baseball card.

TRADE SECRET

Most trading cards, be it baseball cards or the latest Japanese game cards, come in a standard size. To frame these cards, cut the outside of the mat board 3½" x 4½" (9cm x 11cm) with a border of ⅜" (10mm). This leaves an ⅛" (3mm) reveal for the float mat to show.

8 GLUE THE CORNERS AND CARD TO THE FLOAT MAT
Place all four photo corners on the card. Apply a dab of craft glue to the back of each corner (be careful; excess glue may ooze out onto the back of the card). Center the card on the backing and press down on the corners to secure. Repeat for the remaining cards.

9 TRANSFER A LETTER TO THE MAT
Use your computer to create a team letter or enlarge an existing letter from a piece of paraphenalia and trace it onto a piece of paper. Cut out the letter, and place it facedown (backwards) on the back of a piece of mat board cut a bit larger than you'll need. Trace the shape of the letter onto the mat board with a pencil. Remove the letter, then use a ruler and pencil to mark the straight lines and their intersections.

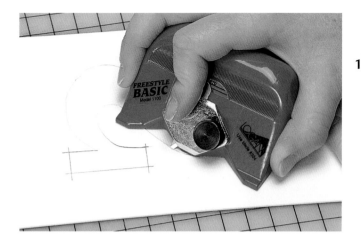

10 CUT OUT THE LETTER

Cut the straight lines using your regular mat cutter. Then using the handheld cutter with the pointed blade, cut the curving lines of the shape. Treat the shape like a square, always keeping the cutter on the inside of the shape. Keep the cutter flat on the table as you manuver it around.

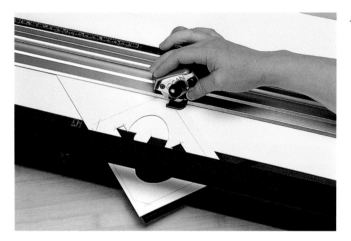

11 CUT AROUND THE LETTER

With a pencil and ruler, create a rectangular box around the letter, on the back side of the mat board, leaving approximately $^3/_4$" (19mm) of space around the cutout. Notch the corners of the rectangle, then use the mat cutter to cut the shape out with a reverse bevel. (See page 34 for more on cutting reverse bevels.)

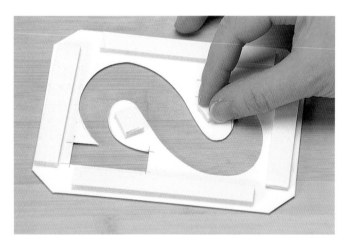

12 BUILD UP THE LETTER

To add dimension to your letter, cut pieces of foam board to fit around the edges of the letter. Glue the foam board to the mat with craft glue.

13 ADHERE PAPER PIECES TO THE FLOAT MAT

Set the baseball mitt on the float mat for placement while you lay out the paper items. Be sure to leave at least $^1/_8$" (3mm) around the edge of the float mat; this will allow enough room for the foam board sides that will be added in step 17. Set the mitt aside. Use glue to adhere the letter and trading cards to the float mat. If the cards overlap, build up the top cards with a layer (or layers) of foam board.

14 MARK A HOLE FOR THE MITT
Place the mitt back into the arrangement. Use a pencil to make a mark between two of the fingers of the mitt, close to where they are joined.

15 INSERT A BOLT THROUGH THE HOLE
Using a drill or Japanese hold punch, punch a hole large enough to accommodate the size of your bolt at that mark. Insert the bolt.

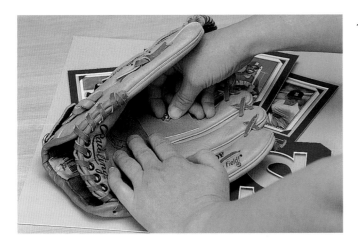

16 SECURE THE MITT TO THE MAT
Place the mitt back onto the mat, with the bolt coming between the finger sections. Cut a small square piece of mat board and drill a hole in it. Place this over the bolt, on the mitt, like a washer. Then place a nut over the mat board and tighten to secure the mitt. If you like, use the needle-nose pliers to further tighten the nut while holding the bolt in the back. If your mounted item has the potential to swivel on the bolt, secure it further with a second bolt or by sewing the piece to the float mat (see page 38).

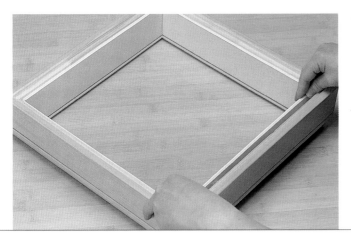

17 CREATE SHADOW BOX SIDES
Clean the glass with glass cleaner and a terrycloth towel. Insert the glass in the frame. Mount scrap pieces of the float mat to foam board. Cut these pieces to a width that's the height of the frame, minus the glass and the float mat. Cut two parallel sides to fit the width of the frame, then cut the other two sides to fit between the first two. Use tape and glue to secure the strips to the inside of the frame. To finish the frame, place the mounted board into the frame and use the point driver to secure. Cover the back with kraft paper and attach a wire to hang (see Putting It All Together, page 27).

11

Creating Depth with Trim Molding

The artwork used for this project did not look quite right with a mat, but the use of either a fillet or simple trim molding turned on end to add depth can be used in any project, mat or no mat.

Cutting one frame to go around another is known as stacking the molding. You can achieve some great looks for your artwork by choosing two moldings that go well together and bring out different elements in your artwork. One small design rule of thumb: Make sure the two you pick are noticeably different in width, or you might end up with a striped look that could be distracting.

WHAT ELSE YOU'LL LEARN

• *How to stack moldings*

ABOUT THE ARTWORK

Marcus the cat has been immortalized in this beautiful colored pencil portrait done for me by the very talented Margaret Hopkins. Because of the stark realism and the direction that Marcus is facing, he appears to me to be looking at something outside of the frame. So in this rare instance, I didn't want to add a window mat.

I didn't want him to look too boxed in or crowded either, so I put some space beween him and the frame by adding depth with the trim molding. The addition of the simple, inner frame also gives the eye a small place to rest and makes the piece look just a bit more finished.

WHAT YOU'LL NEED

two coordinating picture moldings (one will be cut to fit over the other)

small, decorative trim molding

glass, cut to size

miter saw

basic tool kit (see page 11)

finishing hardware

offset clips (with screws)

pencil

acrylic paint

paintbrush

craft glue

kraft paper (for dust cover)

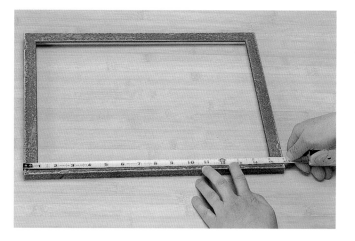

1 DETERMINE THE SIZE OF THE OUTSIDE FRAME
Cut the smaller, inner frame to fit the size of the artwork. Join this frame and then measure the outside of it to determine the measurements at which to cut the outside frame. Add $\frac{1}{8}$" (3mm) to each measurement before cutting. Join the larger frame and set it aside.

2 MAKE THE FIRST CUT ON THE TRIM MOLDING
Cut one end of the decorative trim molding using the miter saw. Place the trim molding up on its side in the miter saw (not flat) and make the first mitered cut.

3 DETERMINE LONG SIDE LENGTH
Set the cut end into the inner frame and mark with a pencil where it should be trimmed on the other end.

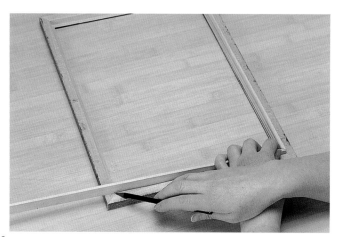

4 DETERMINE THE SHORT SIDE LENGTH
Cut the two long sides, then place them into the frame. Insert one cut end of the molding in the corner, against the mitered piece in the long side. Again, mark the opposite end with a pencil where you need to trim it.

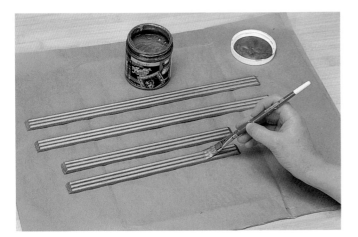

5 PAINT THE TRIM MOLDING RAILS
Remove all the trim molding pieces from the frame. Paint the molding with acrylic antique gold paint, and then let the paint dry.

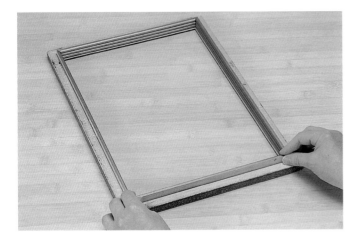

6 GLUE THE PAINTED RAILS INTO THE INNER FRAME
With the glass inside the inner frame, glue the painted rails into the frame. Run a bead of glue along the bottom edge of the back of the trim and dab glue onto the corners. Put the two long sides in first, then glue the ends of the shorter pieces and place them in the frame.

7 STACK THE TWO FRAMES TOGETHER
Attach the smaller frame to the larger frame using offset clips (in this case, ⅛" [3mm]). If the clips are still a little loose, use mat board shims to secure.

8 SECURE ARTWORK WITH MORE OFFSET CLIPS
Brush off the artwork and the glass. Insert the art in the frame, placing it on top of the trim molding. Use screws and offset clips to secure the artwork to the frame, placing the clips about 2" (5cm) apart. To finish the back, tape kraft paper to the back, mitering the corners with a fold (see page 73), and attach a wire for the hanger (see Putting It All Together, page 29).

Alternative Framing Solutions

Now that you've flexed your framing muscle with the traditional techniques of mat cutting, corner mitering and glass cutting, it's time to flex your creative muscle and delve into a new world of possibilities.

Not only will you find that virtually all of the projects in this section can be completed for less than half of the cost of traditional framing, you will see that in most cases you don't even need fancy equipment or tools. Again, it's up to you to decide what you want to put into it. Mitered cuts are very nice, but they're not mandatory. Glass has a beautiful effect over artwork, but so can acrylic and even vinyl (yes, vinyl, that notorious sofa protectant).

Crafters will have a great time in this section. It's all about painting, crackling, sanding, collaging and embellishing. Artists on a budget will find economical solutions to show their work. The myths "I can't afford to frame this" and "I don't have any framing equipment," I'm happy to say, are going to be debunked!

You will find nearly all the materials to complete the projects in this section at your local hardware or home improvement center. Are you skeptical? C'mon, let's get started . . .

Creating a Glass Pocket with Nails

This is a simple solution that incorporates the protection of glass without the need for a standard frame. When searching for a surface on which to mount your glass, if it's flat and you can hammer nails into it, you can use it. Precut lumber is available for hobbyists at most large home improvement centers, and you can always have them cut it to whatever size you desire. This project can be as simple or elaborate as you wish to make it. It's fun, super easy and makes a great gift.

WHAT ELSE YOU'LL LEARN

• *How to wrap a board with paper*

WHAT YOU'LL NEED

metallic, textured 4-ply mat board (optional)

small block of wood

glass, cut to size

decorative paper

decorative brass nails

mat cutter (optional)

ruler (as a guide for nailing)

scissors

brayer

bone folder

hammer

hanging hardware

découpage medium

craft glue

ABOUT THE ARTWORK

Corey Moortgat is like my sister; in fact, people often ask us if we are sisters. This photo of the two of us together always makes me smile and makes me feel like she's right here with me, even though we live thousands of miles apart (2,413 to be exact).

Because the theme of this photo is a wedding, I wanted to use paper that was elegant and stunning and that had color to contrast with the black and white of the photo. I found some Japanese paper that fit the bill perfectly, and the brass nails added a bit of sparkle.

1 APPLY GLUE TO THE FRONT OF THE BOARD

Cut a small mat frame for your photo and set it and the photo aside. (This mat is optional, but I recommend not putting glass directly on your photo. See *Sticky Situation*, page 93.) Cut a piece of paper larger than your wood board. Fold the paper around the board to be sure the paper reaches to the back of the board. Brush a mixture of craft glue and water on the top of the board.

2 CENTER THE BOARD ON THE PAPER

Place the board facedown in the center of the paper. Turn it over and smooth out any bubbles or wrinkles (I like to use a brayer). Then turn the board back over. Wrap all sides of the paper around the board and crease. Notch squares out of the corners for a good fit. Brush the glue and water mixture onto one long side of paper and wrap it around the board.

3 SEAL WITH DÉCOUPAGE MEDIUM

Glue the other long side in the same way, then glue the two short sides around the back of the board. Smooth the paper down everywhere with your fingers or a bone folder. To protect the paper, coat all sides of the board and paper with découpage medium.

4 SCORE AROUND THE GLASS

Cut the glass to be $\frac{1}{8}$" (3mm) wider and longer than your matted image (so that there will be $\frac{1}{16}$" (2mm) of glass around all sides of the image). Position the glass in the desired spot on the board. Score around what will be the bottom and two sides of the glass with a bone folder.

FRAME IT!

5 | MARK HOLES FOR THE NAILS
Use the awl to start nail holes just slightly outside the lines you just scored. Place the holes ½" (13mm) apart around each of the three scored lines.

6 | HAMMER IN THE NAILS TO A CONSISTENT DEPTH
Hammer nails into each of the holes, leaving the head of each nail raised above the board a depth of the mat plus the glass. The distance for this piece is about ⅛" (3mm), so I stacked these two rulers to this height and used them as a guide for nailing.

7 | SLIDE IN THE ARTWORK AND THE GLASS
If you wish to hang this piece, attach a sawtooth hanger or a wire to the back. Clean the glass and stack it with the matted image. Slide everything under the nailheads.

BOARD COVERED WITH TORN BITS OF PAPER

VARIATION

This project is very similar to the one you just completed, but instead of covering the board with one large piece of paper, several smaller pieces of torn decorative paper were découpaged over the board. Standard silver nails replace the decorative brass nails.

STICKY SITUATION

It's never a good idea to place glass directly on a photo you love. Humidity often causes the gelatin in the photo's emulsion to stick to the glass. Once it sticks, you're usually stuck! An art restoration house may be able to soak and salvage your piece, but preventative maintenance is really the key to a photo's longevity, and a simple mat can save you from heartache. If you really don't want a mat, try using acrylic, which is safe to place directly on the photo.

13

Securing an Image to a Board with Acrylic

A simple piece of wood becomes a blank canvas for any sort of paper, paint or combination of the two that you wish to cover it with. This project gives you the creative opportunity to combine framing and collage. The finished product is unlike anything you've seen in a framing gallery. Not only is the project easy, it is so much fun. I love scratching and sanding acrylic to make it look old and weathered.

Consider using this approach to creatively display some of those holiday cards you've been accumulating for years. Try collaging with wrapping paper or festive ribbon. Or combine ticket stubs and other souvenirs from your last vacation with a photo and enjoy that vacation as a piece of art that is displayed year-round. Did I mention that the cost of materials for this solution will have you joyfully laughing all the way to the hardware store?

WHAT ELSE YOU'LL LEARN

• *How to decorate a board with stain, crackle and collage*

ABOUT THE ARTWORK

This photo was taken by my good friend Marissa Bowers on a vacation to Boston. The subject is the USS Constitution from the Revolutionary War, and the inspiration for the poem "Old Ironsides." You can still tour the boat, if you're interested.

I wanted to really play up the nautical theme, so I stained the wood (like a boat) and then dry-brushed it with marine blue paints and crackle medium. The collaged pieces of map carry out the look even further. I like the way that the wood underneath the acrylic looks preserved, while what's been left "outside" appears to be weathered and worn.

WHAT YOU'LL NEED

wood board ($1/2$"–$3/4$" [13mm–19mm] thick)
acrylic (such as Plexiglass), cut to size
collage papers or ephemera
drill
awl
scissors
ruler
sandpaper or a wire brush
paintbrush(es)

wood screws
hanging hardware
paper towels or rag (for stain removal)
pencil
acrylic paint
water-based stain
crackle medium
découpage medium
masking tape

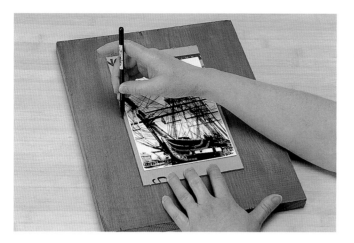

1 TRACE THE ACRYLIC FOR PLACEMENT
Measure your image and cut a piece of acrylic ¼" (6mm) wider than the image and 2" (5cm) longer than the image (see page 22 for how to cut acrylic). Position the acrylic and image on the piece of backing wood (in this case a piece of plywood that I cut and stained). Trace the acrylic with a pencil for placement.

2 APPLY PAINT AND CRACKLE MEDIUM
To keep the portion of the board that will be under the acrylic free of paint, place masking tape along the inside of the pencil line you just drew. Add a second row of tape inside the first, in case you get a little messy. Apply a base color of acrylic paint to the area outside the masked space, using a medium brush. Here I left some of the stained wood showing. When dry, brush on a coat of crackle medium as instructed by the manufacturer.

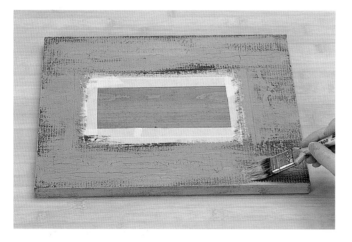

3 ADD A TOP COAT
Brush on the top coat of paint. As the paint dries, the crackles will appear. Again, I didn't apply a solid layer of paint.

4 PREPARE COLLAGE PAPERS
Once the top coat is dry, remove the masking tape. Position your collage elements where you'd like them to be. If any of the papers extend into the stained area, mark the edge of the area with a pencil, then trim the paper to fit.

FRAME IT!

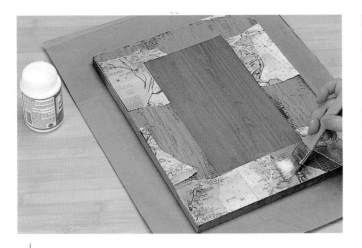

5 | ADHERE PAPERS WITH DÉCOUPAGE MEDIUM
Once the arrangement of your pieces is set, use a brush to spread découpage medium onto the board and then place the collage elements on top. Brush more medium over each of the papers.

6 | APPLY A SECOND COAT OF MEDIUM
After all the pieces are in place, brush over the paper and the entire board with a coat of découpage medium.

7 | DRILL HOLES FOR THE SCREWS
With the protective paper still on the acrylic, use a ruler and a pencil to mark where you'd like the screws to be. Here I placed them $^3/_8$" (10mm) from the top and bottom edges, and evenly spaced across the width. Drill holes large enough to accommodate the screws. In this case I used a $^5/_{32}$" (4mm) drill bit.

8 | ROUGH UP ONE SIDE
Remove the protective paper from one side of the acrylic. Use sandpaper or a wire brush to scratch the acrylic area around the screw holes and a little around the edges to add a bit of texture.

9 | SECURE THE IMAGE WITH SCREWS
Place your main image in the center of the previously-masked area. Remove the second sheet of protective paper from the acrylic and place the acrylic over the image, with the scratched side faceup. Use an awl to make starter holes for the screws. Then use a drill to drill the screws through the holes and into the board. Attach a wire or a sawtooth hanger to the back of the wood to hang.

14

Creating a Vinyl Pocket on Fabric

If you love sewing and working with fabric, this solution will have you right in your element. This is a clever way to coordinate textiles in your room with your framing.

Clear vinyl comes on a roll and can be found at fabric stores. Not only is it good for protecting your footstool from kitty's claws, it makes a great glazing substitute as well! Create one, two or as many pockets as you need, and sew them all onto a piece of inexpensive fabric that you've painted to suit your mood.

I enjoyed sewing these pockets by hand, but a sewing machine would work well too. I liked the natual look of the copper pipe with the patina tones in the painted fabric, but you could substitute a wooden dowel or bamboo instead.

WHAT ELSE YOU'LL LEARN

- *How to paint untreated fabric*
- *How to secure a copper pipe dowel for a hanger*

ABOUT THE ARTWORK

These photos of Dave and me were taken the week we got married. The photos were originally in color, but I scanned them into my computer and changed them to black and white. Because they were taken in an outdoor setting, I wanted to keep the feeling of the overall display natural with tones of copper, green and teal.

WHAT YOU'LL NEED

natural muslin

clear vinyl

copper pipe, cut to size

$1/4$" (6mm) copper caps (to fit ends of pipe)

heavy thread (like coat or carpet thread)

iron

scissors

ruler

needle (or sewing machine)

dressmaker's pins

sawtooth hangers

large flat paintbrush

acrylic paint

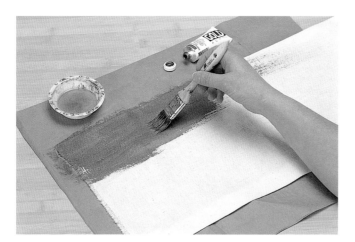

1 APPLY FIRST PAINT COLOR TO THE FABRIC
Cut or tear your piece of muslin fabric to be 1¹/₂" (4cm) shorter than the length of your precut pipe. For my piece I cut the two long sides with scissors (because they will be folded over and won't show), but tore the short sides because I wanted a frayed look. Iron the fabric, then fold over each of the long sides 1" (3cm) and iron the folds flat. Paint the fabric using an acrylic paint and a large flat brush, thinning the paint with water to get a lighter effect in places, if desired.

2 SEW SEAMS FOR THE PIPE
Once the paint is dry, sew the folds down, placing the seams ³/₄" (2cm) from the folded edges of the fabric. To keep my stitches even as I was hand-sewing, I premarked the fabric, making marks ¹/₈" (3mm) apart. You can also use a sewing machine if you're not into sewing things by hand.

3 ADD A SECOND COLOR OF PAINT
Apply a second coat of paint to the fabric to add texture. Go ahead and paint over your stitches if you like. I used a semidry brush for my second color. Set the fabric aside to dry thoroughly.

4 CUT VINYL FOR YOUR IMAGES
Measure your photos. Cut the flexible clear vinyl larger than the photos, adding ³/₄" (19mm) to each side and the bottom; add ¹/₈" (3mm) to the top.

FRAME IT!

5 | BEGIN SEWING VINYL POCKETS ONTO THE FABRIC
Determine the positioning of the vinyl on the fabric (here I left 2$\frac{1}{2}$" [6cm] on each end and centered the third image between the other two). Pin the first piece of vinyl in place. Stitch the sides and bottom of the vinyl to the fabric by hand or with a sewing machine. I used a variegated thread I purchased at a craft store to sew these pieces to my fabric.

6 | THREAD PIPES THROUGH SEAMS
Insert the precut pipes through the sewn channels and put $\frac{1}{4}$" (6mm) caps on all four ends.

7 | ADD SAWTOOTH HANGERS TO FINISH
Sew two sawtooth hangers at the top seam 1$\frac{1}{4}$" (3cm) in from either end. Insert photos into pockets.

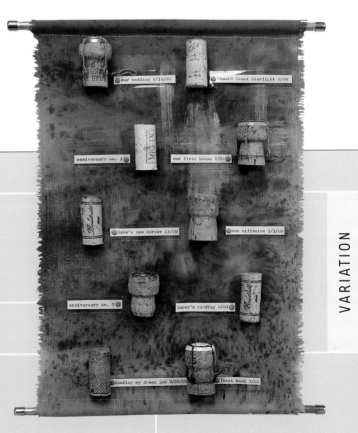

WINE CORK COLLECTION

Wine corks are often saved from special occasions and displaying them all together along with labels identifying each one is much better than keeping them in the kitchen drawer. T-pins inserted from the back secure the corks and acetate protects the computer-generated text labels.

VARIATION

NO. 15

Using a Clipboard as a Frame

A clipboard has the utilitarian job of holding paper, but don't you think it looks cool when it not only holds art, but actually becomes part of the art itself? Another example of a blank canvas just waiting for your clever ideas, a clipboard can be painted, covered with paper or both. Spray paint the board with metallic silver spray and display a contemporary photo on it, or paint it with stripes and have it hold a few of your favorite grandmother's recipes.

The glass here was wrapped with copper tape, but you could leave it unwrapped. Or drill holes through both a piece of acrylic and the clipboard, then sew the two together with colorful embroidery thread.

WHAT ELSE YOU'LL LEARN

- *How to wrap glass in copper tape*
- *How to use tissue paper to create texture*
- *How to add embellishments to glass and frame*

WHAT YOU'LL NEED
masonite clipboard

glass, cut to size

tissue paper

assorted buttons

small piece of copper
(for embellishment)

paintbrush

acrylic paints

paper towel

gel medium

copper tape

epoxy or silicone

craft glue (optional)

ABOUT THE ARTWORK

This project (and the artwork it holds) comes from Corey Moortgat. Corey is a very talented artist and a fellow framer! The inspiration for this partic-ular piece of artwork was the result of a class Corey took from acclaimed artist, Anne Grgich. Because of the artwork's unique style, she didn't want to house it in an ordinary frame, so the idea of an altered clipboard satis-fies this framing need perfectly.

1 BEGIN APPLYING TISSUE TO THE CLIPBOARD
Tear printed tissue paper into pieces that are approximately 4" x 6" (10cm x 15cm). Brush gel medium onto a section of the clipboard and adhere a piece of tissue over it. Brush more gel medium on top of the tissue paper and continue adding more pieces in the same manner.

2 PAINT IN A SOLID BACKGROUND AREA
Cover the clipboard with tissue paper. Let the gel medium air-dry, or use a heat gun to speed up the process. Paint the clipboard with a wash of yellow and white paint, randomly adding color to different areas. Brush a more concentrated mix of these colors in the center to act as a frame for the artwork that will eventually be "clipped" onto the board.

3 SPATTER WITH BROWN AND WHITE PAINT
Thin brown paint with water, place your brush in the mixture, then tap the brush to spatter paint on the surface. Repeat with white paint mixed with water. Soften the spatters if you like by dabbing them with a paper towel.

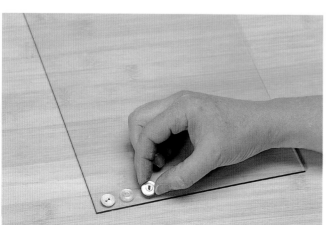

4 EMBELLISH THE GLASS WITH BUTTONS
While the paint dries, cut the glass to 7½" x 10½" (19cm x 27cm). Use craft glue to adhere buttons to the bottom part of the glass.

5 WRAP THE GLASS EDGES WITH FOIL TAPE
Wrap copper tape (available in the stained glass section of craft stores) around the edge of the glass, burnishing it around the edge with your fingernail.

6 INSERT ARTWORK UNDER THE GLASS
Center the artwork on the painted area of the clipboard, then place the decorated glass under the clip.

7 EMBELLISH THE METAL CLIP
Cut a piece of copper and age it by either dipping the metal into a liver of sulfer solution or spatter parts of it with patina shades (blues and greens) of acrylic paint. When dry, glue buttons to the copper piece, then glue the copper to the clip using epoxy or silicone.

8 ADD A FINISHING TOUCH TO THE GLASS
If you wish to give the final piece just a bit more dimension, you can add a line of text or other small elements to the front of the glass with craft glue.

Creating an Acrylic Box for Dimensional Art

This solution is great for artwork that has a bit of depth to it but that you don't wish to mat. I liked the effect of the piece floating between two pieces of clear acrylic, but you could substitute a solid piece of decorated wood (see Framing Solutions 12, page 90, and Solution 13, page 94) or a solid piece of mat board for the backing.

Here the piece of wood that acts as a spacer between the two sheets of acrylic is a simple frame made from trim molding. I mitered the corners, but a frame made with straight cuts would work just as well. The wood that you choose will determine the depth of the box, so measure your piece's height before you head to the hardware store.

This piece was sewn together with wire, but you could also sew it with jute or raffia, or could skip the sewing altogether and secure the pieces with nuts and bolts.

WHAT ELSE YOU'LL LEARN

- *How to use wire to secure pieces together*

WHAT YOU'LL NEED

acrylic sheets (2)

trim molding frame (use molding that is flat on all sides)

20-gauge black wire

ruler

pen

drill

sawtooth hangers

acrylic paint or water-based stain

adhesive transfer tape

artist's tape or masking tape

ABOUT THE ARTWORK

If you're thinking this fabric art looks like the work of Claudine Hellmuth, you're right! Claudine has told me that she has a reluctance to use power tools, so I hope this all-manual-tool framing solution will inspire her to explore new frontiers when displaying her truly inspirational works.

Because her piece was quilted, I wanted to not only show off its texture but also carry out the stitched theme. The wood spacer between the acrylic keeps the artwork dimensional, and the wire sewn around the outside continues the "frayed-edges" style.

1 MARK THE HOLES FOR DRILLING

Cut two pieces of acrylic to the same size. On one piece, place marks on the protective paper for the holes you will use for sewing, making marks on all four sides. Here I placed marks 1/4" (6mm) from the outside edge and spaced the marks 1" (25mm) apart. The first and last holes of each side are placed 1/2" (13mm) in from the corner.

2 CREATE A FRAME TO FIT INSIDE THE ACRYLIC

Cut and make a frame (see pages 23-26) to fit between the two pieces of acrylic, using molding that is 3/4" x 1/2" (19mm x 13mm). Paint or stain the frame as desired. Sandwich the frame between the two layers of acrylic, lining the edges up as well as you can. With artist's tape, tape the pieces on all four sides to secure, making sure the piece marked from the last step is facing out so you can see it.

3 DRILL ALL OF THE MARKED HOLES

Use a small drill bit, such as the 3/32" (2mm), to drill through the three layers at each of the marks made in step 1. Drill onto a piece of scrap wood to protect your work surface.

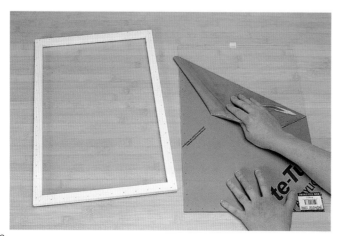

4 REMOVE THE PROTECTIVE PAPERS

Remove the tape. Disassemble the sandwich and remove the protective papers from the acrylic. Use artist's tape to mark the pieces so you know what order they were stacked in. I usually mark the outside top of each piece.

FRAME IT!

5 APPLY TAPE TO THE BACK OF THE ARTWORK

Place adhesive transfer tape on the back of the artwork. Burnish the tape well with your fingers to secure to the artwork before peeling off the back of the tape.

6 ADHERE THE ARTWORK TO THE ACRYLIC

Center the frame on the back piece of acrylic. Position the artwork on the acrylic "backing" and press firmly to secure.

7 BEGIN SEWING WITH THE FIRST PIECE OF WIRE

Place the top piece of acrylic over the frame. Use wire to sew the three pieces together, cutting pieces of wire about 24" (61cm) long (or vary the lengths if you like). Thread the wire through the first hole, leaving a tail of about 2" (5cm). Sew a whip stitch around the frame to secure everything together. To make a whip stitch, thread the wire through the top of each hole, wrapping the wire around the side of the frame to get to the top of the next hole.

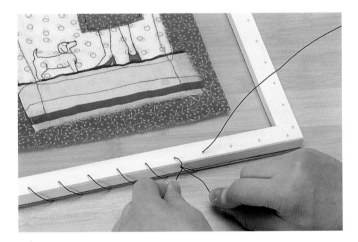

ADHESIVE ALTERNATIVE

If you don't wish to apply tape to your artwork, you could sew it down by first drilling holes through the acrylic in a few spots underneath where the artwork will be placed.

8 CONNECT WIRE PIECES TO CONTINUE SEWING

When you have about 3" (8cm) left of the first piece of wire, cut a second piece and twist one end of the second to the end of the first piece. Trim the ends and continue sewing. (To help keep the sandwich aligned, after the first length of wire is sewn, cut another piece and sew it on the opposite side of the first.)

When you get back to the starting point, secure the last piece of wire to the first by twisting the ends together and trimming. To hang the picture, secure a sawtooth hanger to the center of the back piece of acrylic along the top of the frame. Use a drill and nails to secure the hanger or glue with silicone.

Mounting a Double-Sided Image

Many times the items that you want to frame will be two-sided. Rather than sacrifice the "less-important" side, try this approach and show both sides! Unlike glass, acrylic can breath, so it's safe to have right up against your artwork.

    This piece can either be hung on the wall or propped up on a mantle for easy handling and viewing. Springs are what secure the artwork here, but you could also hang the piece from cable strung to the top and bottom. Another alternative is to substitute a metal frame (cut to the same size as the acrylic) for the trim molding and use spring clips, which hide in the channel (see page 51, step 14), to secure the piece.

WHAT ELSE YOU'LL LEARN

- *How to use trim molding as a frame*
- *How to use alternative hardware to secure artwork in a frame*

ABOUT THE ARTWORK

I found this letter at the antique market and thought it was one of the cutest things I had ever seen. I just love the tiny envelope and the voice of the little boy who composed the letter. It was very important to me to be able to read the entire letter, so both sides had to be visible.

    Because the letter was written by a child, I thought the use of springs as hardware added a bit of whimsy.

WHAT YOU'LL NEED

acrylic sheets (2)

trim molding, cut to size

strap clamp

ruler

pencil

drill

needle-nose pliers

awl

clothesline wire

screw eyes (6)

tiny nuts and bolts (6 each)

springs (6)

basic tool kit (see page 11)

foam brush

water-based stain

paper towels or rag (for stain removal)

large marker (or similar round shape)

artist's tape or masking tape

wood glue

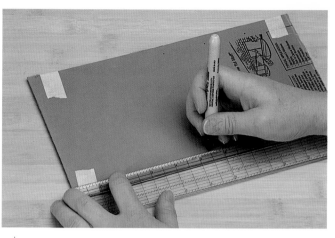

1 CUT AND STAIN THE MOLDING

When determining your frame size, plan on leaving about 4" (10cm) of space on either side of the artwork, and 3¼" (8cm) at the top and bottom. Cut pieces of trim molding to size, mitering the corners. Stain the pieces to your liking, using a water-based stain and a foam brush. Before the stain dries, use a paper towel to wipe off the excess. Turn the pieces over and stain the back of the molding as well.

2 MARK HOLES TO BE DRILLED

While the frame pieces dry, cut two pieces of acrylic that will leave about ¾" (19mm) of space around all sides of your artwork. Leaving the protective paper on the acrylic, tape the pieces together. Along each long side mark a total of five holes: one in the center, one 2" (5cm) from the top and one 2" (5cm) from the bottom, and two more holes, centered between the end holes and the center hole. Place each mark about ½" (13mm) from the edge. Center one hole on the top and bottom sides, ½" (13mm) from the edge.

3 DRILL ALL OF THE HOLES

Using a drill bit that will make holes to fit your particular bolts and wire (in this case ³⁄₃₂" [2mm]), drill the holes where marked. Drill with the acylic over a piece of scrap wood to protect your work surface.

4 COIL WIRE TO FORM JUMP RINGS

To make uniform jump rings, wrap clothesline wire around a large marker or similar shape. Make as many loops as you'll have springs, six in this case, then add one more.

5 CUT LOOPS APART FOR RINGS

Use wire cutters to cut each loop apart, for a total of six rings. Try to cut the wire at an angle to make joining the ends together easier.

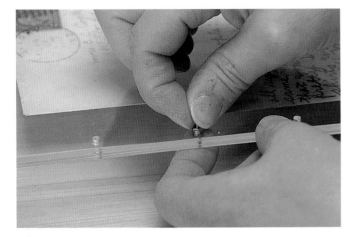

6 SECURE ARTWORK BETWEEN ACYLIC PIECES
Make a mark with tape as to which two sides of the acrylic were drilled together, to keep alignment correct. Remove the protective papers from the insides of the acrylic, then sandwich the artwork between the two clear sides. Remove the other pieces of protective paper and double-check the position of the artwork. Insert the bolts and nuts, placing the nuts on the front or back, whichever you prefer. Start with the holes on the top and bottom, then place two on each side, leaving the three alternating holes for the jump rings.

7 JOIN THE FRAME
When the stained pieces of molding are dry, glue the corners together and place in the strap clamp to set until the glue has cured (see page 24). Once dry, nail the corners (see page 26).

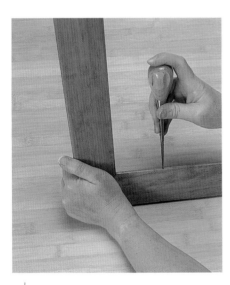

8 MARK HOLES FOR THE SPRINGS
Decide where you'd like to attach the springs to the inside of the frame. Make marks with a pencil at these points, then use an awl to begin the holes. Here, the first hole on each side is 2" (5cm) from the top, the next is 3½" (9cm) from the first, and the third is 7" (18cm) from the second.

9 SCREW SPRINGS INTO THE FRAME
Attach a spring (in this case, I used 3" [8cm] springs) to a screw eye, and screw it into the first hole marked on the side of the frame. Once you have the screw in, use the nail set to tighten it. Repeat for the other five springs.

10 SECURE SPRINGS TO JUMP RINGS
Place the acrylic piece in the center of the frame. Thread a jump ring into each hole in the acrylic, then attach a spring to the jump ring. Use needle-nose pliers to close the jump rings. Attach a sawtooth hanger to the top of the frame if you wish to hang the piece on the wall.

Creating a Nonmitered Frame

For paintings that are stretched on a strainer or stretcher bar, all you really need to frame them are four strips of wood. I chose to add a frame of trim molding that was attached to the top of the painted lumber, but you could forgo that step if you wanted to.

If you choose to paint your wood to match the painting, like I did for this project, look for colors that are dominant rather than those that aren't as visible. If you want a natural look, try staining the wood instead of using paint.

WHAT ELSE YOU'LL LEARN

- *How to frame a canvas*
- *How to build a frame with inexpensive lumber*
- *How to paint your frame to match your artwork*

ABOUT THE ARTWORK

Using water-soluble oil paints, James A. Markle created this piece, entitled Lunken Breeze, from a sketch that was taken on location. Preferring to use color as an expression of mood and movement, the artist was able to record one of his favorite places—a park where this majestic tree overlooks a small airfield.

When deciding on a paint color for the wood that would frame this piece, I wanted to continue the breezy feel of the painting with tones of blue that matched the artwork. The whitewash treatment also reflects the texture of the paint.

WHAT YOU'LL NEED

$1/2$" x $1^{1}/_{2}$" (1cm x 4cm) lumber

1" x $3/16$" (3cm x 5mm) trim molding

strap clamp

ruler

awl

cutting mat

sandpaper

finishing nails

hammer

hanging hardware

acrylic paints

paintbrush

wood glue

1 | CUT THE SHORT RAILS FIRST
Cut two lengths of wood to fit the short sides of the canvas. To determine the length of the long sides, measure the length of the canvas with the addition of the two short pieces of wood.

2 | PAINT THE WOOD TO MATCH THE ARTWORK
Cut the long sides to length. Paint the frame pieces to complement the artwork. Here I painted the pieces with a medium blue first, let that dry, then lightly brushed white paint over it, using a dry brush. Applying the paint with a dry brush gives the frame a distressed effect.

3 | GLUE THE SIDES OF THE FRAME TOGETHER
When the paint has dried, set the wood pieces in place around the canvas, then loosely set the strap clamp around the painted pieces (see page 24). Apply glue to the ends of the short rails, then tighten the strap clamp around the pieces and canvas, gluing the frame together.

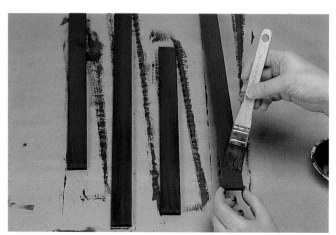

4 | CUT AND PAINT TRIM MOLDING
Set the clamped frame aside to dry. Once the glue is dry, cut pieces of trim molding to fit on top of the frame. Align the molding with the inside edge of the frame to determine the length needed for each side. Then paint the top pieces to complement the artwork. When these are dry, sand the edges a bit to distress them.

FRAME IT!

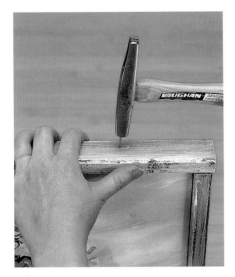 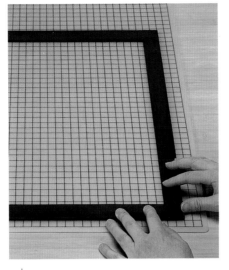 

5 | NAIL THE FRAME TO THE CANVAS
While the top pieces dry, nail the frame to the canvas. Use an awl to mark the nail holes, then hammer in the nails. Use a nail set to countersink the nails into the frame. Two nails on each side should suffice.

6 | GLUE THE TRIM MOLDING TOGETHER
Glue the four sides of your trim molding together. Align on a cutting mat to make sure it's square.

7 | ATTACH THE TRIM PIECE TO THE FRAME
Spread wood glue on the top of the frame and glue on the trim molding. Weight it down with a piece of glass, if necessary. Secure wire to the back of the frame to hang (see Putting It All Together, page 27).

VARIATION

MESH-WRAPPED MOLDING

For additional texture on your simple wood molding, try wrapping the individual pieces with gutter screening before gluing the rails together. A staple gun works well to secure the mesh to the wood, and any sharp edges can be flattened with a hammer.

19

Using Hardware Pieces to Create a Frame

This solution can satsify the urges of your inner construction worker! Joining wood with metal plates is as visually interesting as it is functional. This type of project is the perfect way to use wood that is cosmetically flawed or generally unappealing, because it is completely hidden by the hardware on the surface.

In the case of this project, I think the frame really does become art in and of itself, which some might see as a distraction. But I see it as an opportunity to create something extremely unique.

Another approach to take would be to paint the plates with a color of metal spray paint. You could paint the frame either after or prior to adding the screws, depending on whether you'd like the screws to be a contrast or more of a subtle element.

WHAT ELSE YOU'LL LEARN

• *How to use embellishments to enhance a frame*

ABOUT THE ARTWORK

While I was working on this piece of art, I was imagining it would be framed with a white mat and a silver frame. But when I tried setting the piece on this black corrugated mat board, I knew I had found a winner. Because of the silver wire (and just because I love silver), I still thought it needed a silver frame, but I wasn't exactly thinking of stainless steel!

I've always loved the industrial look, and I had some of these mending plates in my studio from a previous art project. It occured to me that I could place several of them together to make a dramatic frame. I think the effect is perfect. Now I'm anxious to try other shapes and combinations of plates.

WHAT YOU'LL NEED

$3^{1}/_{8}$" x 7" (8cm x 18cm) mending plates (6), available in the lumber section of hardware or home improvement stores

$1^{1}/_{2}$" x $^{3}/_{4}$" (4cm x 19mm) lumber

acrylic, cut to size

$^{1}/_{8}$" (3mm) eyelets

colored brads

wood glue

wood screws

small tack nails

finishing hardware

hammer

hand drill or screwdriver

eyelet setter

awl

paintbrush

black acrylic paint

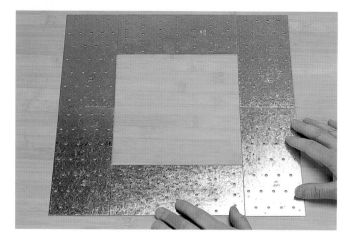

1 DETERMINE THE FRAME SIZE
Lay out the mending plates to plan the frame size you will want. Mending plates come in a variety of sizes. I prefer using these large ones, but use whatever size you like.

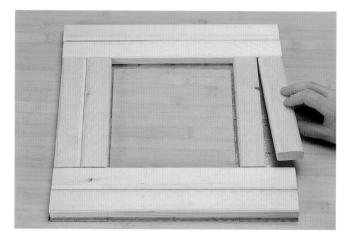

2 CUT WOOD PIECES TO FILL IN BEHIND THE PLATES
Using 1$\frac{1}{2}$" x $\frac{3}{4}$" (4cm x 19mm) wood strips, cut enough wood to back the mending plates. You should have about $\frac{3}{16}$" (5mm) overhang for the plates on the inside. This will serve as a lip for the glass and the artwork.

3 PAINT THE WOOD PIECES
Use acrylic paint to paint the wood pieces. Set aside to dry. I chose black, so the effect would be for the pieces to "disappear."

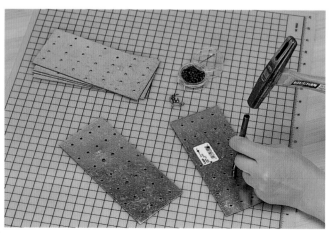

4 EMBELLISH THE PLATES AS DESIRED
Attach brads through the holes in the mending plate, using a hammer to flatten the flanges on the back. Set eyelets into the holes in the mending plate, using an eyelet setter and a hammer. To do this, place the eyelet through the front of the plate, then turn the plate over. Place an eyelet setter into the shank of the eyelet and use the hammer to tap the setting tool, which flares the shank and secures the eyelet. Remove the setting tool and tap the hammer to the back of the eyelet to further flatten. Repeat for all the mending plates, creating a pattern of brads and eyelets as desired.

FRAME IT!

5 GLUE ALL OF THE WOOD TOGETHER
Arrange the painted wooden pieces on your work surface as you had originally cut them. Use wood glue to attach the pieces together.

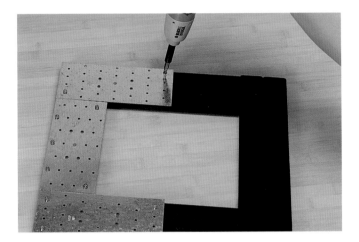

6 SECURE THE PLATES TO THE WOOD WITH SCREWS
Position the mending plates on the frame. The plates are slightly wider than the pieces of wood, so position the pieces so that they are flush with the outside of the wood. Use an awl to mark the holes for the screws, then drill the screws into the holes in the mending plate.

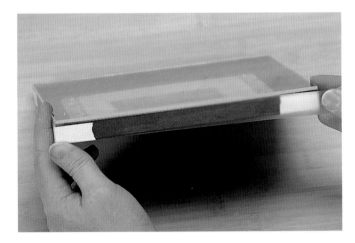

7 PREPARE ARTWORK AND GLASS
Insert the glass and the artwork into the frame. I created a folded shadow box around my artwork (as shown in Framing Solution 5, page 52). I cut the acrylic to the size of the shadow box and taped it to the top of the box to secure. Because the frame has a lip, you can just insert a piece of acrylic or glass and place the artwork against it, instead of creating the shadow box.

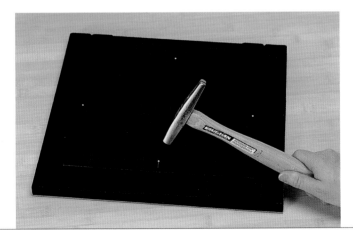

8 NAIL THE ARTWORK INSIDE THE FRAME
Secure the artwork to the frame with a point driver, or you can cut a piece of mat board larger than the opening for the artwork and nail the mat board to the back of the frame, as I'm doing here. Place a nail on each side to position the board, then add more nails to secure tightly. Attach a sawtooth hanger or wire to hang.

20

Building a Frame Around an Acrylic Box

An acrylic box is useful when your artwork has significant depth to it. This solution is an inexpensive answer to a custom-built Plexiglas box.

As with all of the projects in this book, and especially in this section, other options for this solution are numerous. The width of the wood could be altered as could the type of hardware.

One key to remember is that the artwork or the mat board that the art is floated on should be $1/8$" (3mm) larger on all sides than the printed size of the plastic box. This will allow the artwork to rest on the edge of the box and not go inside of it.

WHAT ELSE YOU'LL LEARN

- *How to cut nonmitered frame sides*
- *How to distress a painted frame*

ABOUT THE ARTWORK

I liked the idea of using an acrylic box for this piece of artwork because it let in more light and really made it easy for the viewer to see what was "going on." Because I love using nuts and bolts, I also liked the fact that you could see both sides of them using this approach.

The clean lines of the wood and the shine of the box create a contemporary, almost urban, look that complements the high energy of this piece.

WHAT YOU'LL NEED

ready-made acrylic box frame

$3/4$" x $1^1/2$" (19mm x 4cm) lumber

drill

strap clamp

needle-nose pliers

sandpaper

nuts and bolts (10 each)

finishing hardware

paintbrush

acrylic paint

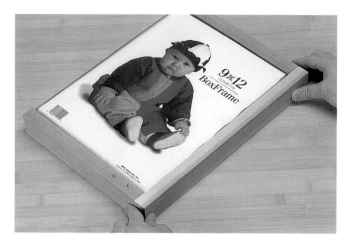

1 CUT THE WOOD TO FIT THE BOX
Cut your wood to fit the outside of the ready-made box. Cut the short sides first to the exact width of the box, then cut the long sides so they extend the entire width of both the box and the ends of the short sides. Do this with the short sides in place.

2 PAINT THE WOOD
Paint the wood to complement the artwork. Add a second coat if necessary for complete coverage. Allow to dry before continuing.

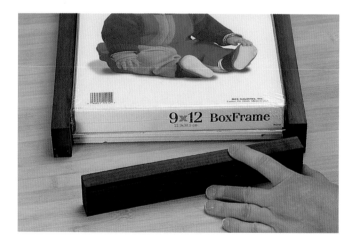

3 CUT FOAM BOARD TO LIFT BOX
You can choose to either have the plastic box flush with the top of the wood, or you may wish to have it raised a bit to create additional depth. To lift the plastic box, cut three pieces of foam board to $9\frac{1}{8}$" x $12\frac{1}{8}$" (23cm x 31cm). Set the three pieces of foam board under the box, then assemble the frame around the box and the foam board. This will keep the box level and in place while you drill the holes into it in the next step.

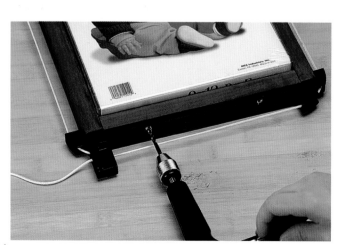

4 DRILL HOLES IN WOOD AND BOX
Use the strap clamp to hold the frame together. With a pencil, mark where you will drill your holes: two on the short sides and three on the long sides. Space the holes evenly along each side. Drill the holes on the sides, drilling through the wood and the plastic box.

5 DISTRESS THE FRAME
Clean up the plastic chips and wood shavings from the frame pieces and from inside the plastic box. Before you attach the frame pieces, distress them by sanding the edges. Keep track of which piece goes where as you're sanding.

6 INSERT BOLTS
Insert bolts through the holes on the inside of the plastic box. Hold the bolts in place, then place the wood pieces onto the bolts. Start with the two short sides, then attach the two long sides.

7 SECURE ARTWORK IN FRAME
Hand-screw the nuts onto the outside of the frame to secure the bolts. After all the pieces are in place, tighten the nuts with needle-nose pliers. Place your artwork in the box. Use a point driver to secure if the back of the artwork is lower than the frame. Here I had mounted my artwork on a wood frame. Since the two frames were flush with each other, I used a staple gun to secure the artwork in place.

VARIATION

BIT BY BIT

Hard plastic, such as that which ready-made acrylic boxes are typically made of, has a tendancy to crack easily when you try to drill into it with a large drill bit. To avoid this frustration, start with a small bit, such as a $^3/_{16}$" (5mm) bit, and work up progressively larger from there. A power drill usually works better than a hand drill if you choose to "risk it" and just start with the large bit.

LONGER LONG SIDES

An easy way to add interest to your nonmitered frame is to cut two of the opposing rails (in this case, it was the long sides) so that they extend beyond the other two opposing rails. There is no rule of thumb as to how much longer they should be; it's entirely up to you.

Resources

Most of the materials used in this book can be found at your locate framing shop, craft or art store or at a hardware or home improvement store. If you can't find an item, contact the manufacturer listed below for a retailer near you.

CRESCENT CARDBOARD COMPANY, L.L.C.
100 W. Willow Road
Wheeling, IL 60090
(800) 323-1055
www.crescentcardboard.com
• mat board

THE FLETCHER-TERRY COMPANY
65 Spring Lane
Farmington, CT 06032
(800) 843-3826
www.fletcher-terry.com
• plastic and glass cutters
• point driver, framer's points

LARSON JUHL
3900 Steve Reynolds Boulevard
Norcross, GA 30093
(800) 886-6126
www.larsonjuhl.com
• picture frame molding

LINECO INC.
P. O. Box 2604
Holyoke, MA 01041
(800) 322-7775
www.lineco.com
• linen tape
• photo corners
• archival glue

LOGAN GRAPHICS PRODUCTS, INC.
1100 Brown Street
Wauconda, IL 60084

(800) 331-6232
www.logangraphics.com
• framer's saw
• board-mounted and hand-held mat cutters

NIELSENBAINBRIDGE
40 Eisenhower Drive
Paramus, NJ 07653
(800) 526-9073
www.nielsen-bainbridge.com
• metal molding
• Artcare mat board and foam board

SPECIALTY TAPES
Division of RSW Inc.
4221 Courtney Lane
Franksville, WI 53126
(800) 545-8273
www.specialtytapes.net
• artist's tape
• framer's tape

3M
3M Corporate Headquarters
3M Center
St. Paul, MN 55144
(888) 364-3577
www.3m.com
• adhesive transfer tape
• spray adhesive

TRU VUE
Division of Apogee Enterprises, Inc.
9400 W. 55th Street
McCook, IL 60525
(800) 621-8339
www.tru-vue.com
• regular and conservation glazing products, including Acrylite acrylic

Index

A-C

acrylic glazing, 11
    cutting, 22
    distressing, 97
    dusting, 27
    securing with screws, 94-97
    securing with wire, 108-109
        see also Box frame
adhesive transfer tape, 10
adhesives, 10
allowance, 23
artist's tape, 10
artwork, 8
    positioning, 19
    securing, 19-20
awl, 11
backing, 9
    building up, 39
bevel, 8
    reverse, 34, 35
black-core mat board, 8
box frame, 122-125
canvas, frame for, 114-117
corner vise, 25
countersink, 26
cutting mat, 22

D-F

depth, adding, 68-73, 84-87
double mat, 18, 45
dust cover, 28, 73
fabric
    as frame, 98-101
    painting, 100
fillet, 70-71
    as frame, 74-77
finishing hardware, 12
float mat, *see* Float Mount
float mount, 13
    collectibles, 78-83
    dimensional items, 67, 76, 82, 83
    with thread, 38
    with wire, 72
foam board, 9

acid free, 9
    adhesive-backed, 9
frame, 16, 23-29
    between acrylic, 106-109, 110-113
    breaking down premade, 44
    clipboard, 102-105
    cutting, 23
    decorating, 96-97, 104, 116, 117, 118-121, 125
    determining size, 15, 16
    determining style, 16
    for dimensional artwork, 52-57, 64-67, 68-73, 74-77, 78-83, 106-109, 122-125
    for double-sided artwork, 110-113
    fabric, 98-101
    fitting, 27-29
    joining, 23-25
    metal, 50-51
    nailing, 26
    nonmitered, 114-117, 122-125
    wood board, 90-93, 94-97
framer's knot, 29
framer's points, 12
framing solution, 7
French lines, 34-35

G-L

glass, 11
    anti-reflective, 11
    cleaning, 27
    conservation, 11
    cutting, 21
    decorating, 104-105
    dusting, 27
    reflection-control, 11
    scoring, 21
    securing with nails, 92-93
glazing, 11. *See also* Glass, Acrylic.
glue, 10
hangers, 28-29, 99
jump rings, 112

M-P

mat board, 8

4-ply, 8
8-ply, 8
    as backing, 9
    cutting, 17, 54
    cutting a double mat, 18
    cutting, decorative, 49, 65-66
    cutting, freehand, 81-82
    cutting, multi-opening, 48, 54
    cutting, octagonal, 41
    decorating, 32-35, 44, 62
    determining color, 13-14
    determining size, 15
    fabric, 9, 40
    fabric wrapped, 60-61
    metallic, 9
    patterned, 9
    textured, 9
mat cutter
    bench cutter, 17
    handheld, 17, 82
    slip sheet, 18
measuring, 13, 48
miter box, 23
miter saw, 23
molding. *See* Frame, Trim molding.
museum board, 8
nail set, 11
nails, finishing, 12
offset clips, 12, 73
photo corners
    acid-free, 10, 20
    making your own, 80-81
photographs, protecting from glass, 93
picture wire, 12
point driver, 11, 12, 27

Q-S

rabbet, 12
rag board, 8
reveal, 9
reverse bevel, 34, 35
sawtooth hanger, 12
scoring glass, 21
scratch awl, 11
screw eyes, 12

screws, 12
shadow box, 52-57, 74-77, 78-83
    building up sides, 77
    folded sides, 54-55
    from ready-made frame, 69-73
silicone, 10
spray adhesive, 10, 20
spring clips, 51
strap clamp, 24
strap hangers, 12

T-Z

T-hinge, 19
tac hammer, 11
tape
    adhesive transfer, 10
    artist's, 10
    framer's 10
    gummed linen, 10
textiles
    fabric as frame, 98-101
    mounting, 37-41
    stretching, 62-63
trim molding, 84-87
weighted bottom, 15
white-core mat board, 8
wire, 12, 29
wood screws, 12

Get creative with North Light Books!

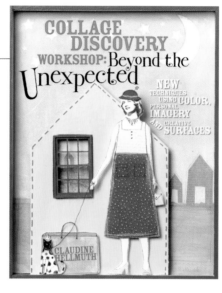

Whether you're a beginner or a collage veteran, you'll love this book for both its practical how-to information and its inspirational artwork. Inside you'll find original artwork and inventive ideas that show you how to personalize your own collage pieces using new techniques and unique surfaces. An extensive gallery of pieces by the author and other top collage artists is sure to spark your imagination.
ISBN 1-58180-535-7   paperback   128 pages
33267-K

With intriguing paper projects that go beyond basic cards and gifts, this book will show you how to turn ordinary home items into extraordinary, stylish pieces. Inside you'll find projects for crafting accents for every room in the house and easy techniques for transforming lampshades, clocks, tabletops and more.
ISBN 1-58180-656-6   paperback   128 pages
33243-K

Let Tera Leigh act as your personal craft guide and motivator. She'll help you discover just how creative you really are. You'll explore eight exciting crafts through 16 fun, fabulous projects, including rubber stamping, bookmaking, papermaking, collage, decorative painting and more. Tera prefaces each new activity with insightful essays and encouraging advice.
ISBN 1-58180-293-5   paperback   128 pages
32170-K

Designed to inspire friends to gather around the table, break out the projects and create with abandon, *Wild with a Glue Gun* offers a stunning array of craft projects, while showing craft clubs and other small groups how to foster an atmosphere of creative sharing.
ISBN 1-58180-472-5   paperback   144 pages
32740-K

These books and other fine titles are available from your local art & craft retailer, bookstore, online supplier or by calling 1-800-448-0915.

FRAME IT!